Ex Oriente Lux et Veritas
Yale, Salisbury, and Early Orientalism

Portrait of Edward Elbridge Salisbury
by George Augustus Baker, Jr., 1871
Collection of Yale University

Ex Oriente Lux et Veritas
Yale, Salisbury, and Early Orientalism

———

Karen Polinger Foster, editor

Yale Babylonian Collection Occasional Papers 1

New Haven, Connecticut

2017

ISBN 9780692824276

TABLE OF CONTENTS

Acknowledgments

In 2016–2017, Yale University celebrated the 175th anniversary of its appointment of Edward Elbridge Salisbury as the first professor of Arabic and Sanskrit in America. A complete listing of the symposia, exhibitions, and other commemorations that took place may be found on the website, salisbury175. yale.edu.

The present volume publishes expanded versions of the papers delivered at the symposium "Edward Salisbury and the Ancient Near East," held on 4 November 2016. It is a pleasure to acknowledge here the able assistance of Marwa Khaboor, Lora LeMosy, and Arturo Perez-Cabello in ensuring that the event arrangements ran so smoothly. Support for it was provided by the Yale Babylonian Collection, the Viscusi Fund of the Department of Near Eastern Languages and Civilizations, and the Council on Middle East Studies.

The book has benefited from the advice and efforts of many, especially John Gambell, Yale University Printer, and Judith Ann Schiff, Yale University Chief Research Archivist, who shed light and truth on the iconography of the Yale blazon; Peter W. Johnson, Yale Graphic Designer emeritus (see About the Cover); Carl Kaufman, Babylonian Collection photographer, who took the splendid images of the cylinder seals published in Appendix II; Agnete Wisti Lassen, who coordinated publication and distribution matters; and Peter Machinist, who read a draft of the manuscript with his usual care and kindness.

About the Cover

The cover, designed by Peter W. Johnson, Yale Senior Graphic Designer emeritus, in collaboration with the editor, unites many of the themes and ideas represented in the contributions to this volume. Aesthetically, it evokes the Orientalizing hues and chromatic combinations of the nineteenth century, while the mosaic squares remind us of the tile work so characteristic of Islamic decorative arts.

The Yale blazon, on the blue used regularly as the school color since the 1860s, has a complicated iconography, conceived in the early eighteenth century as the central device on the Yale seal. Two words from the Hebrew Bible, Urim and Thummim, appear on an open book, presumed to be the Bible, accompanied by the Latin phrase Lux et Veritas, light and truth. While their precise meaning is often debated, Urim and Thummim are here usually taken to refer to the oracular gems worn by the high priest Aaron. According to a divinity textbook studied in eighteenth-century Yale, the words prefigured the New Testament and denoted the light and perfection of Jesus Christ and his oracular will. How perfection became Veritas involves Yale's stand on the divisive theological issues of the day.

Over the years, the Yale blazon has undergone numerous design variations, from the elaborate renditions of the past to the linear simplicity of the current model. The cover version is from the 1930s, chosen for the pictorial relevance of its scrolls and laurels. Of special note for the present volume is the fact that the earliest extant example of the seal's use is the impression on the 1749 master's diploma of Ezra Stiles, who, as Yale's president from 1778 to 1795, taught Hebrew and could read both Jewish mystical texts (kabbala) and a simple Arabic historical text (if he had a translation before him).

The image of Salisbury derives from a photographic portrait made in his later years. As part of the logo designed for the 175th anniversary celebration of Salisbury's appointment (back cover), it was drawn by Patrick Lynch, Yale's Senior Digital Officer for Design, Analytics, and Social Media.

Next to Salisbury is a detail of a cuneiform text that appeared in Carsten Niebuhr's 1778 account of his journeys to the Middle East, where, among other things, he copied this royal inscription at Persepolis. Its publication led to the successful decipherment of Old Persian, and ultimately to those of the other ancient languages written in cuneiform script.

On the left below is a detail of one of the many Arabic manuscripts that Salisbury bought in Paris at the 1842 estate auction of the library of Silvestre de Sacy and donated to Yale in 1870. The flyleaf is signed E. Scheidius (an eighteenth-century Dutch Orientalist and theologian). The manuscript attests to Salisbury's interest in Arabic belles-lettres, for it is a copy made in 1206 of the Maqamat, a tenth-century literary work by al-Hamadhani. It is housed now in Yale's Beinecke Rare Book and Manuscript Library (Salisbury MSS 63).

The last square shows a detail from a notebook kept by Salisbury's student William Dwight Whitney. In this one, also in the Beinecke Library (GEN MSS 1125), he was working on a translation of the Atharvaveda, a collection of 20 books containing 730 hymns. Whitney copied out the Sanskrit, adding his comments about the source manuscripts and the collations he had made in European libraries.

Salisbury and Yale
Karen Polinger Foster

In mid-September of 1828, at the age of fourteen, Edward Elbridge Salisbury journeyed from his native Boston to New Haven, where he presented himself for the oral examination required for entrance to Yale College.[1] As F. A. P. Barnard, who went on to be president of Columbia, described his own experience in 1824, "the applicants for admission were divided into squads of moderate numbers each. Mine consisted of eight victims besides myself."[2] A faculty member posed questions on Greek and Latin authors, geography, and arithmetic. Young Salisbury was deemed sufficiently prepared, thanks to a short stint at the Boston Latin School and prior home tutelage by his merchant/clergyman father.[3] In late October, he returned to New Haven as a member of the class of 1832.

Thus began a quarter-century of direct association with Yale, and decades more as a loyal benefactor and supporter. While others in this volume and elsewhere have discussed Salisbury's contributions to the birth of Orientalist scholarship in America, the following brief remarks aim to give a picture of what Yale was like when he was a student (1828–1836) and faculty member (1841–1856). These were critical years in the institution's history, and Salisbury played no small role in its transition from college to university. Reciprocally, its evolving curricular and pedagogical precepts and practices shaped his professional trajectory and outlook.

When Salisbury matriculated, along with some ninety fellow freshmen, Jeremiah Day (Yale 1795) had been president since 1817, steadily transforming the school into a place for a "thorough education."[4] This was defined in the 1828 *Report of the Course of Instruction in Yale College by a Committee of the Corporation and the Academical Faculty*, which set forth rationales for what would endure as the core principles of liberal arts education in the United States.[5] Intellectual development and mental discipline, it held, were more important than training in particular or practical areas responsive to the needs of the moment. To these ends, the *Yale Report*, as it is usually called, reaffirmed the lasting value of the dead languages of Greek and Latin, decried by many as useless, irrelevant subjects in an America poised on the threshold of the industrial age. Yet at the same time, and this is its far-reaching contribution, it opened the way for adding new fields of study, provided that they demonstrated their potential for enlarging a student's capacities for analytical thought and creative analysis.

With the *Yale Report* freshly issued, Salisbury and his classmates spent their first three years following a prescribed program: Greek, Latin, mathematics, history, astronomy, geography, general science, and English grammar and rhetoric. Senior-year course choices included metaphysics and ethics, composition, and belles-lettres, as well as offerings in French, German, Spanish, chemistry, and political economy.

Recitation was the standard pedagogical mode. The memoirs of Julian M. Sturtevant, class of 1826 and long-serving president of Illinois College, castigate the faculty, who "could hardly be said to teach at all, their duties being to subject every pupil three times a day to so searching a scrutiny before the whole division as to make it apparent to himself and all his fellows either that he did or did not understand his lessons."[6] Students were expected to be completely self-reliant in mastering the material, although some instructors did provide explanations of errors and encouragement for those failing to recite adequately. Benjamin Silliman, the renowned professor of chemistry, exceptionally taught in ways akin to modern methods, for he lectured, did experiments, and used rock specimens as exhibits in his mineralogy course. But mainly the faculty drilled, rather than inspired. When the Latin professor remonstrated after finishing Tacitus that the class had read "one of the noblest productions of the human mind without knowing it," Sturtevant recalled that he and the other students "might justly have retorted, 'Whose fault is it?'"[7]

Day was determined to improve this situation by turning the *Yale Report*'s ideals and philosophy into reality. In 1830, halfway through Salisbury's undergraduate years, Day introduced the concept of faculty specialization. Barnard had been awed when Silliman examined him and the other candidates in "Virgil, Cicero, the Greek Testament, Graeca Minora, Xenophon, Geography, and Arithmetic, all apparently with equal facility."[8] But the time had come, Day believed, for Yale instructors to teach the one or two subjects in which their true competence and enthusiasm lay. This injected rigor and vigor into the curriculum, and went hand-in-hand with raised admission standards.

Student protests erupted, coalescing around the new requirements for geometry. The Conic Section Rebellion of 1830, as it is known, resulted in the expulsion of 43 of the 96 members of Salisbury's class. They had refused to take the final exam, for it included mandatory, individual drawing of geometric figures, which previously students had been able to reference in the textbook. Five years before, smaller protests ended when the students involved were reinstated after they signed a statement recognizing college authority in all such matters. This time, however, nearly half the class of 1832 was rusticated, with the further step that letters were sent to peer institutions, asking that the dismissed not be admitted to finish their degrees. Fifty years later, Salisbury, as Class Secretary and on behalf of the alumni of 1832, requested that Yale consider awarding honorary degrees to his expelled classmates, many of whom had in fact enrolled elsewhere and achieved professional eminence.[9] This was done for some, but not all, who were still living.

Beyond the classroom, Salisbury's fellow students were prone to acts of disruption and violence. On campus, they engaged in elaborate pranks, such as ingeniously vandalizing the clock in the tower of the Lyceum classroom building, or spiriting away the faculty's pew cushions to feed bonfires.[10] They also regularly staged public complaints, as in the Bread and Butter Rebellion of 1828, about the quality and variety of the food served in the dining hall. From 1806 until the custom was banned in 1840, a College Bully was elected to lead his compatriots in fights with New Haven youths or in brawls with sailors who had put into New Haven harbor, one of the busiest in New England.[11] As did Salisbury, many of these roisterers excelled academically and later had distinguished careers, but from what we can tell of him, he was an observer or abstainer, not a participant.

Architecturally, Yale likewise underwent significant change during Day's 29-year presidency.[12] Along the west side of the New Haven Green stood the Old Brick Row of classrooms, dormitories, and chapel, separated from the town by wooden railings known as the Fence. Under Day's aegis, three buildings were added to the Row, but with the construction of the Cabinet in 1819, the Trumbull Gallery in 1832, and the Library in 1842, the college began to look inward on its own quadrangle. In addition to this shift, the trio signaled new educational directions for the college, and they made a striking visual break with the uniformly red, stylistically homogeneous Row.

The Cabinet was a handsome, stuccoed building with Ionic pilasters. Its second floor housed the 10,000-piece mineral collection of Colonel George Gibbs, which he had loaned to Yale in 1812. A dozen years later, he declared his desire to take his collection back and sell it for an asking price of $20,000. Yale did not hesitate, despite lacking funds for the purchase. Day managed to raise half the sum and to persuade Gibbs to hold notes for the balance. Added to the 2000 specimens Yale already owned, as well as the spectacular chunks gathered in 1807 from the Weston, Connecticut meteor fall, the Gibbs Cabinet made Yale the foremost American center for the study of geology and chemistry.

No sooner had this been bought than Colonel John Trumbull announced that he would give Yale his iconic Revolutionary War paintings in exchange for a lifetime annuity. Day urged Yale to seize the opportunity to build a gallery, the first American art museum connected with a college. Trumbull designed a Greek Revival structure of light-colored stone, originally with no upper windows, for it was also to be a crypt for the artist and his wife. In due course, the museum's presence gave rise to the first School of the Fine Arts to be part of a college, which opened in 1869 and admitted the first women at Yale.

From the beginning, Salisbury was among the Gallery's staunchest supporters. One senses his presence behind the scenes in Yale's acquisition of four reliefs and assorted objects from the newly discovered ruins of the Assyrian palace of Assurnasirpal II at Nimrud.[13] These were obtained by the Reverend William Frederick Williams, a missionary in nearby Mosul. His Yale ties included brief attendance in 1838 and a brother and nephew on the faculty. Reaching New Haven in 1854, the large stone slabs were seen as tangible proof of the biblical prophecies of the downfall of Assyria, thereby serving as a monumental "recruiting poster for the Divinity School at Yale."[14] The Mesopotamian cylinder seals that arrived with the reliefs were published by Salisbury in 1856; the first full study since then is offered here in Appendix II.

The last big capital project of Day's administration was the Library, which anchored the western edge of the campus, tilting the college further away from the Green. The first Gothic Revival building at Yale, by 1846 it had over 10,000 volumes and a full-time librarian who kept it open for four hours daily except Sundays. In addition to contributing to the Library's building fund, Salisbury in 1870 donated his important collection of Arabic books and manuscripts. Over the years, he also gave Yale material in Turkish and Persian, much of which had come to him through his extensive contacts with American missionaries working in the Middle East.

In 1846, Yale decided to think seriously about organizing graduate studies, beyond what existed in the Departments (later Schools) of Medicine, Law, and Theology. Salisbury served on the committee that recommended forming a new Department, to be called Philosophy and the Arts. This began in the fall of 1847 with such courses available as general philology (Josiah W. Gibbs), Pindar (Theodore Dwight Woolsey, Yale's new president), and psychology (Noah Porter, who would succeed Woolsey). For his part, Salisbury proposed "instruction in Arabic grammar and points on relations of Arabic to other Shemitish dialects."[15] At the Yale commencement in 1861, doctoral degrees were conferred for the first time in the United States.

Two of Salisbury's graduate students went on to brilliant Yale careers—James Hadley in Greek and William Dwight Whitney in Sanskrit. The diary Hadley kept from 1843 to 1852 affords a glimpse of Salisbury as a teacher.[16] In the evening of 11 February 1850, for example, he and Whitney had a Sanskrit class, after which Salisbury "spoke very freely," asking if they "preferred going on" by themselves. Hadley thought not, believing that classwork was mutually beneficial: for the student, "new views…and the responsibility of the lesson"; for the professor, "the discipline of teaching, which every teacher knows to be invaluable." Above all, Hadley writes, what Salisbury does "gives body to his department, making it…not a mere name or abstraction, as some are apt to suppose of a Sanskrit and Arabic professorship."

Despite these worthy arguments, in 1851 Salisbury tendered his resignation, was induced to withdraw it, and then in 1853 definitively gave up his Sanskrit post in favor of Whitney. Three years later, he relinquished his professorship in Arabic. According to Hadley's diary entry for 2 August 1851, "he is morbidly modest and this plays the mischief with him." He had insisted, for example, that he should teach without compensation ($1100–$1500 annually in the period)[17] and this was duly noted in his 1841 letter of appointment (Appendix I). Furthermore, during his lifetime, he gave a fortune ($130,000, nearly $4 million today) in gifts and collections, as well as an endowed professorship in Sanskrit and a substantial contribution to a chair in natural history, but he was adamant that none of his benefactions should bear his name. No major Yale donor of the nineteenth century was so self-effacing. In 1871, he did sit (reluctantly, we imagine) for his portrait, commissioned in appreciation for his donation of the Arabic books and manuscripts.[18] Fittingly, this now hangs in the American Oriental Society room in Sterling Memorial Library and is reproduced, for the first time, as the frontispiece to the present book.

Salisbury died in New Haven in 1901, the year of Yale's bicentennial. Officially a university since 1887, the institution to which he had steadfastly devoted his counsel, intellectual energies, and resources was thriving under the progressive leadership of Arthur Twining Hadley, son of his Sanskrit student a half-century before. Today, Salisbury would recognize only two buildings from his student and faculty days—South Middle College (Connecticut Hall), sole vestige of the Old Brick Row, and the Library (Dwight Chapel)—but he would doubtless be gratified that his legacy is alive and well, from the scores of doctorates earned in Arabic, Assyriology, and Semitics in the Department of Near Eastern Languages and Civilizations to the vibrancy of the Yale Babylonian Collection to the university's lasting commitment to teaching and learning about the "Orient."

NOTES

1. For biographical information, see Benjamin R. Foster, "Edward E. Salisbury: America's First Orientalist," *Al-'Usur al-Wusta: The Bulletin of Middle East Medievalists* 9.1 (1997): 15–17 and his Salisbury entry in the *American National Biography* (1999 edition), vol. 9: 206–8.

2. Quoted in Brooks Mather Kelley, *Yale: A History* (New Haven: Yale University Press, 1974), 156. This, the standard work on Yale's first 275 years, is the source from which much of the following material derives.

3. Salisbury wrote an unassuming autobiography for the class book he edited, *Biographical Memoranda Respecting All who Ever Were Members of the Class of 1832, Yale College* (New Haven: Tuttle, Morehouse & Taylor, 1880). In it, he attributes his lifelong diffidence to having been schooled at home until age 12, when his father died.

4. A concise account of Day's career and accomplishments appears in Reuben A. Holden, *Profiles and Portraits of Yale University Presidents* (Freeport, Maine: Bond Wheelwright Co., 1968), 63–68.

5. For a recent assessment of this document, see Jurgen Herbst, "The Yale Report of 1828," *International Journal of the Classical Tradition* 11.2 (2004): 213–31.

6. Quoted in Kelley, *Yale*, 159.

7. Quoted in Kelley, *Yale*, 161.

8. Quoted in Kelley, *Yale*, 157.

9. Salisbury, *Memoranda*, Appendix.

10. Holden, *Yale: A Pictorial History* (New Haven: Yale University Press, 1967), captions to illustrations 26, 28.

11. Floyd Shumway and Richard Hegel, eds., *New Haven: An Illustrated History* (New Haven: New Haven Colony Historical Society, 1981), 63–75.

12. Images and descriptions of all Yale buildings to 1966 may be found in Holden, *Pictorial History*.

13. Sam Harrelson, *"Asia Has Claims Upon New England": Assyrian Reliefs at Yale* (New Haven: Yale University Art Gallery, 2006).

14. Susan B. Matheson, *Art for Yale: A History of the Yale University Art Gallery* (New Haven: Yale University Art Gallery, 2001), 29.

15. Quoted in Kelley, *Yale*, 183.

16. Laura Hadley Moseley, ed., *Diary (1843–1852) of James Hadley: A New Haven Journal* (New Haven: Yale University Press, 1951). Salisbury regularly taught and received students at home, a stately Tuscan Revival mansion designed and built for him about 1839 by Ithiel Town and Alexander Jackson Davis (1934 view preserved in the New Haven Free Public Library, Local History Room, Photograph Collection). This may have been the first residence Town and Davis did in the Tuscan style (Roger Hale Newton, *Town & Davis Architects: Pioneers in American Revivalist Architecture* [New Haven: Yale University Press, 1942], 248). The renowned architects' many projects in New Haven made the city the "Athens of Connecticut" (Elizabeth Mills Brown, *New Haven: A Guide to Architecture and Urban Design* [New Haven: Yale University Press, 1976], 5). Salisbury's house and large garden occupied the northeast corner of Church and Wall Streets, now the site of the new (1971) New Haven County Courthouse. Opposite were the houses of his brother-in-law, Theodore Dwight Woolsey, and his mother, both standing today, although much altered (250 and 258 Church Street).

17. George Wilson Pearson, *A Yale Book of Numbers: Historical Statistics of the College and University, 1701–1976* (New Haven: Yale University, 1983), 599–600.

18. Franklin Bowditch Dexter, *A Catalogue, with Descriptive Notices, of the Portraits, Busts, etc. Belonging to Yale University, 1892* (New Haven: Tuttle, Morehouse & Taylor, 1892), 93. About the time of his presentation at the court of Louis Philippe and the birth of his daughter in 1837, Salisbury was persuaded to sit in Paris for a miniature on ivory by Jean-Baptiste Isabey, favored portraitist of French notables, whose rendering showed him "possessing peculiar charm and distinction," according to Mary Perkins Quincy, "Edward Elbridge Salisbury," *New England Historical and Genealogical Register* 55 (1901): 362. In his declining years, he posed for several studio photographs, one of which hangs today in the Yale Babylonian Collection.

Orientalism's Lonely Years:
The Case of Edward Salisbury
Suzanne Marchand

It has long been my conviction that we can learn a great deal about 'Orientalism' by listening not to its theorists, but to its practitioners. Let us begin, then, with some words written in 1843 by Edward Salisbury, whose contributions we are assessing, for the first time, in this collection. On this occasion, he was taking up Yale's first chair in Oriental studies, a position that would require him to give instruction in both Indo-European and Semitic languages, and to cover, by himself, the cultures ranging from Tokyo to Tangiers, and from ca. 3000 BCE to essentially the present day—a mandate, I might say, not all that different from that of my senior colleague John Henderson, who was Louisiana State University's *only* historian of the non-West between 1977, when he arrived, and 2006, when we at last hired another scholar in East Asian history. In his inaugural address, Salisbury, predictably, dealt with what we would now call the relevance question, which he defended in the following way: we Americans cannot continue to be ignorant of the East, he wrote, because

> ...the very peculiarity of our national destiny, in a moral point of view, calls upon us not only not to be behind, but to be even foremost, in intimate acquaintance with Oriental languages and institutions. The countries of the West, including our own, have been largely indebted to the East for their various culture; the time has now come when this debt should be repaid. I have imagined, it may have been one end of Divine Providence in giving to our sacred Scriptures a coloring so highly Oriental as they have, to remind the nations of Christendom of their special obligations to the East....

This is the language of Christian supercessionism, but it also includes, as we see clearly in the next passage, an undertone of critique of the West, for its arrogance and intolerance of things Oriental:

> What should Christendom do less than to reflect the glory of the West upon those eastern skies, now pale and shrouded with the world's declining day? Yet what has been rendered to the east by western nations, as such, but

disesteem, treacherous use of its political weaknesses, religious animosity? And these, promoting ignorance, have increased the alienation.[1]

Salisbury was eager, as we shall see, to use knowledge not to reinforce power relations but to *decrease the alienation* of the East. He believed it his mission to explain the beauty of Arabic poetry to those who had reviled it as unworthy of the name, and to refute charges that Muhammed was a deceiver or an epileptic. He hoped that his work would fill in historical lacunae left gaping by European historians who failed to appreciate the high medieval civilizations in the East in which the Arabs were "not only the preservers, but the enlargers of science, the only nation that could be called really civilized, for several centuries."[2] He was certainly a Christian, convinced of the special moral excellence and destiny of the ancient Israelites, and I shall note below his striking prediction, in this 1843 text, that Christianity may have to ready itself for a new set of clashes with Islam. But taking the substance and tenor of his address as a whole, it is evident that Salisbury felt that his Oriental studies made him not a champion of Christian culture, but a rather lonely man. "I will do," he concluded, "what may be in my power to attract others into [Oriental studies], though I am aware I must expect to labor, for a time, almost alone. I would earnestly ask of all of you…to allow me to find refuge from the feeling of loneliness and discouragement in your sympathizing recognition, that each department of knowledge is truly kindred with every other…"[3] Salisbury's rhetoric is that of the supplicant, not the victor, the outsider, not the company man. What can we learn, then, by listening to this lonely Orientalist?

In this essay, I have no intention of painting Edward Salisbury as a hero or a villain of our time; from my point of view, there are some distressing as well as some admirable aspects to his words. But we must remember that his world is not our world, for many reasons, perhaps the most neglected of which is that Salisbury and his fellow Orientalists cared so much more about the *ancient* Orient than do most area specialists today. His world, too, was one that boasted a far different institutional and political landscape, one in which America was not a world power, and virtually all of those who studied 'the ancient Orient' did so in pursuit of clerical careers. The few who wanted to study the ancient Orient beyond the Hebrew Bible, like Salisbury, were compelled to do so in Europe, and depended heavily on British, French, and German scholarship. In fact, Salisbury himself felt greatly dependent on and indebted to the European 'Oriental Renaissance' of the 1820s and 1830s[4]— the latter the period in which he studied in France and the Germanies—and we can learn a great deal about the form of 'Orientalism' he brought to Yale by filling in some aspects of this European backdrop. The object, here, is not to praise or blame Salisbury, who is, after all, long buried, but to get us to understand more clearly his efforts, and those of his contemporary Orientalists, not to reify or 'other' the Orient but to overcome some of its alienation from the West and to appreciate a bit more his loneliness.

In his infamous tirade titled *Black Athena*, Martin Bernal also identified the 1820s and 30s as the moment at which the 'Ancient Model' of civilization's history, in which the Greeks had depended on the Egyptians for much of their culture, was replaced by a racially driven 'Aryan Model,' in which all of western cultural history was rooted exclusively in the 'Greek miracle.'[5] Bernal's argument is full of flaws, perhaps the most serious of which is its complete obliteration of the internal developments in Oriental and classical scholarship that enabled this shift to obtain intellectual legitimacy. But for various reasons, I have come to believe Bernal was quite right about the importance of these decades, decades that saw the victory of anti-Revolutionary reaction, the Greek War of Independence, and the institutionalization of neoclassical educational systems. To fill in the picture more fully, however, we need to take a wider chronological angle and to explore in a bit more detail the prehistory of what I will be calling Orientalism's 'lonely years.'

In the eighteenth century, on the whole, being an Orientalist was *not* a lonely business for a number of reasons. The first is that classicists and Orientalists, or theologians and Orientalists, were often one and the same; many scholars wore all three hats. The second is that in the age of either the old ecclesiastical history or the new universal history, no one thought the ancient Hebrews, Chinese, Persians, Egyptians, and Assyrians could be left out. The third is that mythology, etymology, and chronology—all subjects later subordinated to history or philology—remained relatively autonomous and powerful fields of controversy and investigation, and the Orient was in all cases central to their pursuits. The fourth is that new commodities, manuscripts, and ethnographic reports kept the pot stirring on subjects such as the secrets of Chinese porcelain making, the antiquity of Egypt's kingdoms, and the number of Indian women committing sati. In the era before the deciphers, this was a relatively open discussion, involving characters such as Voltaire, Bishop William Warburton, Newton, and the polymath astronomer C. F. Dupuis, author of the twelve-volume sensation *l'Origine de tous les cultes* (1794). There were forest-killing fights about whether or not China was a colony of Egypt, or the Pentateuch a rip-off of some ur-ancient

Indian shastahs.[6] It was all very confusing and to biblical loyalists both provocative and frightening. We can say one thing: the Orientalists of this era were very often amateurs or polymaths, missionaries or travelers, iconoclasts or defenders of the faith—but they were certainly *not* lonely.

Yet several things were happening by the 1790s, at least, that gave Oriental studies a more dubious place in Europe's cultural-institutional landscape. The first was the mastering of Sanskrit by British scholars, something that gave later eighteenth-century Orientalists the opportunity, as Thomas Trautmann noted years ago, to claim deep knowledge *and appreciation* of the culture of the Hindus than had been previously afforded them.[7] Scholars expected other decipherments—of cuneiform, Avestan, and, above all, hieroglyphs—to follow quickly, and were keenly disappointed when they did not. At a time in which J. G. Herder and the members of the Académie des Inscriptions, among many others, longed for the Orient's 'veil' to be lifted, Oriental studies still chiefly had to be pursued by depending on Greek, Roman, and biblical texts. Most of its practitioners, too, remained theologians or at least members of theological faculties. Difficulties were exacerbated by William Jones's denunciation of Anquetil's Zend Avesta as a forgery,[8] something that set Persian studies back at least three decades, and revelations that Voltaire's veda *was* a fake. In 1784, Herder lamented, "The archives of Babylon, Phoenicia, and Carthage are no more: Egypt was in its decline, almost before a single Greek visited its interior. Everything has been shrunk down to a few faded pages, containing fables of fables, fragments of history, a dream of the prehistorical world."[9] Oriental prehistory had become a fable, one whose riddles even Herder had almost given up trying to solve.

In the meantime, however, classical scholarship was also undergoing a revolution, one that led to its specialization, academization, and its lopping off of religious questions and cross-cultural chronological studies and ety- mologies, subjects that had been absolutely central to all humanistic work in the eighteenth century.[10] Academic classical philologists in France and in Germany, for different reasons, stopped teaching biblical exegesis, and by 1830, also stopped teaching universal history. Skeptics turned their attention away from mythology and prehistory in favor of incisive study of trustworthy texts. Quite suddenly, classics asserted itself as the queen of the secular sciences, and left Oriental studies with the flotsam and jetsam left over from the breakup of the theological faculties, including the answering of all of the very difficult questions such as 'Were the Jews the first monotheists?' and 'What did the Greeks borrow from the Orient?' While classicists now distanced themselves from the work of polymaths, universal historians, and 'mere' travelers, given the complexity of the fields and the incompleteness of decipherments and collections, Orientalists after the 1790s still depended upon or were themselves travelers, missionaries, priests, or poets. This was a real issue: we tend to forget that none of the 'Egyptologists' Napoleon sent to Egypt knew any Oriental languages, except Paradis de Venture, who died there of dysentery in 1799. Edmé-François Jomard, who copied the hieroglyphs and saw the *Description* into print, was a surveyor; his key antagonist in the 1820s, Jean-Antoine Letronne, began his career as a painter in J. L. David's studio.[11] Specialization in this world was vital to further philological progress, but the linguistic knots were very hard to unravel. As late as 1836, Christian Lassen was still complaining that work in ancient Persian languages remained essentially "an etymological blind-man's bluff."[12]

By the 1820s, too, there were fewer gentlemen or clerical scholars with the means and leisure time to pursue arcane subjects such as the untangling of older and younger Avesta. But, even given the background of expanding empires, the Orientalists could not make the case for the relevance of Oriental studies convincingly enough to university or school administrators to obtain academic posts for themselves. Thus those who did get posts ended up having to cover all of the many bases left open by the defection of the classicists. In the early nineteenth century, Orientalists had to learn far more languages than their classicist counterparts: Friedrich Rückert claimed to know fifty, but probably Heinrich Ewald's ten or twelve was more accurate and typical.[13] At Yale, Salisbury's teaching portfolio included a wide range of both Indo-European and Semitic languages, at a time, moreover, when no one else in the United States, to our knowledge, was able to read either Sanskrit or classical Arabic. He wrote essays on Islamic theology, Nestorian monuments, the Chinese origins of the compass, the decipherment of cuneiform, and the history of Buddhism.[14] The consequences of this asymmetrical specialization cemented into institutions of higher learning in the 1790s-1830s echoed through the nineteenth century, and could still be felt in my colleague's career at L.S.U. in the early 2000s.

Something else was troubling the waters of Oriental studies by the 1820s, which might be rather crudely characterized as a new phase in the dialectics of Enlightened and Christian thought. The first turn in this spiral began already in the mid-eighteenth century, perhaps even already in Newton's lifelong project aimed at undercutting all too ancient (and thereby biblically problematical) Egyptian dates by proposing a hugely complicated synchronization of classical, Oriental, and astronomical chronologies.[15] In the wake of Voltaire's attempt to use deep Vedic or Chinese dates to displace the centrality of the Jews in universal history, all sorts of projects sprang up to reconcile biblical chronologies and new Oriental findings, including, as Trautmann describes, William Jones's Mosaic ethnology. This religious reaction was already underway in Britain, France, and the Germanies before 1789, but efforts expanded massively after about 1802—tellingly the date of Napoleon's Concordat—in France, and also in the Germanies.[16] The first decade of the new century was littered with grand projects intended to save the concept of revelation by harnessing it to sprawling Oriental histories; Friedrich Schlegel's "Language and Wisdom of the Indians" of 1808, written on the heels of his conversation to Catholicism, is one good example. It is noteworthy that this was the treatise that converted William Jones's 'Japhetic' language tree into what would be the foundation for Bernal's 'Aryan Model,' and that it was an essay written, for once, by someone who actually could read Sanskrit.

Schlegel's essay was followed by a series of other Romantic universal histories that turned the eighteenth-century's attacks on 'priestly conspiracies' upside down, most famously the Heidelberg polymath Friedrich Creuzer's *Symbolik und Mythologie der antiken Völker, besonders der Griechen*, of 1810-12. Creuzer's *Symbolik* put the origin of all the cults in the East, first in Egypt and, in its second edition, in India and Persia. Creuzer's Neoplatonic diffusionary history drew on the work of his friends Friedrich Schlegel and Joseph Goerres, and was enormously influential, touching classicists, geographers, Orientalists, and theologians alike. Creuzer's history *might* have been the foundation on which a history of civilization that linked East and West, and in which religion was at the center of cultural life, could be built. Perhaps it was for that reason— as well as for its scholarly deficiencies—that by 1821, Creuzer's work was under attack, as a Graecophile and positivist version of Enlightened thought sought its revenge.[17]

It is worth spending just a moment on the so-called Creuzer Affair, as I believe the reaction to Creuzer's Romantic, religion-saving Orientalism was central to the process Bernal described as the demise of the Ancient Model of classical dependency on the East. Creuzer was attacked first of all by the highly respected, but cantankerous, translator of the *Iliad* and *Odyssey*, Johann Voss. Voss was a Graecophile liberal and a vehement critic of Catholic reaction, something he saw exemplified in Creuzer's Neoplatonism. He was horrified by Creuzer's insistence that religion lay at the heart of Greek myth and that this 'irrational' core was, in turn, a reprocessed version of what Oriental priests had been dispensing to their Egyptian and Persian flocks from time out of mind. He was horrified by Creuzer's philosophical and intuitive, rather than purely philological, method.[18] In books and articles, drawing on the advantages gained by the asymmetrical specialization I described above, Voss and his colleagues attacked Creuzer's politics, religion, scholarship, and personal behavior, tarnishing his reputation and nearly resulting in his firing from the University of Heidelberg on charges of being a secret Papist.[19] Some of Creuzer's friends tried, rather halfheartedly, to defend him—but quickly gave up the game. For one thing, Creuzer himself could not read Oriental languages other than Hebrew. He had trusted texts that turned out to be forgeries, and he had made etymological mistakes. Ancient Persian studies, in particular, was far too slender a reed upon which to build any lasting argument. In fact, one of the few specialists in the field, J. G. Rhode, professor at the Royal War College in Breslau, took Creuzer to task for wearing classicizing glasses: Creuzer had started with Greek and Roman myths, and then sought their ancestors in the Orient, Rhode charged, rather than working from the other direction. Rhode, whose specialty was Persian religion, emphasized, instead, the necessity of studying each religious tradition in its own context.[20] The classicist Karl Otfried Müller, similarly, in 1825 penned a treatise on how to study Greek myths with a telling Kantian title: *Prolegomena to a Scientific Mythology*. Müller's claim was that most Greek myths had local and national origins and purposes; Greek mythology, and mythologists, spoke not to universal history, but to the internal history of the Greek nation.[21]

That this was the way the wind was blowing—in favor of studying discrete national traditions rather than 'universal' ones—meant that by the mid-1820s, Creuzerian Romanticism was definitely out. Creuzer himself retained his post, but was thoroughly sidelined; others who had written wide-ranging histories like his own, including the geographer Carl Ritter and the theologian F. C. Baur, turned to more positivistic and specialized studies. By the 1830s, in Prussia, Leopold von Ranke, F. C. Dahlmann, and J. G. Droysen had all given up teaching universal history in favor of teaching national and especially Germanic histories.

A related cultural change that deeply affected Oriental studies was the waning of the age of Romantic poetry. One of the things Oriental studies still had going for it in the 1810s was its very strong connection to Romantic poetry. Many of the leading German Orientalists of the century's turn were themselves accomplished and respected poets. Herder himself was already given to composing 'Nachdichtungen' or imitations of Oriental poetry, but after him came Friedrich and August Wilhelm Schlegel and Friedrich Rückert, all poets who studied Oriental languages chiefly in order to perfect their poetry. We have forgotten how greatly late enlightened Europeans esteemed Sanskrit, Persian, and Arabic poetry; there were many studies of the subject, and extensive translations, of the *Sakuntala*, of the *Bhagavad Gita*, of the *Shahnameh*, of the *Ramayana*, of Hafiz and Ghazzali—many of them translations in verse. Even those Orientalists who were not poets themselves all wrote about or translated poetry—including William Jones, Joseph Hammer (later Hammer-Purgstall), Christian Lassen, Gustav Weil, Silvestre de Sacy—and they did so out of appreciation for its beauty and elegance. Naturally it was this context that spawned the now most cited Orientalizing product of the period, Goethe's *East-West Divan* (1814–18), written under the spell of Joseph Hammer's translation of Hafiz. The Romantics thought poetry the highest art form, and one close to revelation, and the fact that the Orient had mastered the poetic arts spoke volumes about its right to count as a civilized and spiritual place.[22] But by the 1830s, on the continent and in England, new, more literalist forms of Protestant exegesis, and the more cynical and 'realist' novels and plays of Stendhal and Balzac, of Georg Büchner and Willibad Alexis, of Dickens and Fanny Trollope, had begun to make this sort of affection for Oriental poetry seem outdated. Although Orientalists continued to translate Oriental poetry throughout the century, translation of the great Persian or Indian works, or of the Hebrew Bible itself, was no longer seen as preparation for writing 'universal' poetry, or as a key to unlock the mysteries of the human soul.

This, then, is the backdrop against which in 1837 Edward Salisbury came to Europe. He would have found a world in which to speak the name of Creuzer was virtually a taboo, and Romantic affection for 'Oriental' poetry had become embarrassing. Painstaking Greek studies were the order of the day. At that time, Max Müller bitterly recalled, scholars, and especially classicists

> would not believe that there could be any community of origin between the people of Athens and Rome, and the so-called Niggers of India…No one ever was for a time so completely laughed down as Professor Bopp, when he first published his *Comparative Grammar of Sanskrit, Zend, Greek, Latin, and Gothic* [vol. 1: 1833; SM]. All hands were against him; and if in comparing Greek and Latin with Sanskrit, Gothic, Celtic, Slavonic, or Persian, he happened to have placed one single accent wrong, the shouts of those who knew nothing but Greek and Latin, and probably looked in their Greek Dictionaries to be quite sure of their accents, would never end.[23]

This was a world backing away from, rather than seeking to 'conquer' the ancient Near East. Student numbers were small; in 1825, the most renowned German Orientalist, A. W. Schlegel, had only three students in his Sanskrit course.[24] Fortunate enough to obtain an appointment at the University of Erlangen—perhaps eager to have their own version of Schlegel—in 1826, the poet Friedrich Rückert could boast seven students in 1827, but only six in 1828, and one in 1830. Few took note when he retired in 1849, embittered and isolated.[25]

The Orientalists of the age also had to deal with severe poverty and small, often bitterly divided, communities. Christian Lassen, A. W. Schlegel's most promising Sanskrit student, started his work on the *Ramayana* in 1822; in 1824 and 1825, he had to beg a haughty and hectoring August Wilhelm for money to stave off his creditors. Despite collaborating with Eugene Burnouf on a breakthrough book on the Pali language in 1825, Lassen did not gain a modicum of financial security until his appointment as extraordinary professor at the University of Bonn in 1830. In letters to Burnouf and Schlegel, Lassen described just how paltry interest in Sanskrit was in England and France in the 1820s; in England, he wrote, Thomas Colebrooke was the only one who still devoted energy and seriousness to study of Indian literature, while in France, the older Orientalists Chezy and Langlès were hostile to the newer scholarship, so much so that they actively tried to sabotage the work of the more friendly Abel Rémusat.[26] Max Müller might have starved but for the patronage of Baron Bunsen; Bunsen's patronage alone also made possible the careers of Richard Lepsius (Egyptology), Martin Haug (Avestan studies), and Paul de Lagarde (Coptic and Armenian studies).[27] It took a very long time, and usually political intervention, to get these scholars real jobs. Orientalists of Jewish extraction were, of course, even more disadvantaged in the job search. For example, Theodor Benfey spent twenty years in the academic wilderness before receiving a post, and it took an additional fourteen for him to get a chair.[28] But even lonelier than the Jews were those who studied the extra-biblical Far East. The English Sinologist Thomas Manning, who moved to Canton to learn Chinese in 1807, found no support for his endeavors even from the British East India Company and was refused a position at the East India Company College. The one head of state who evinced any interest in his work was by the time of their meeting an equally lonely man, Napoleon, whom Manning visited at St. Helena.[29]

The collection and exhibiting of Oriental materials was no less lonely an endeavor in the century's first decades. There were, of course, funerary obelisks and Egyptianizing home furnishings, and in revolutionary France a few public fountains; but the number of even phony Oriental works pales in comparison to the 800+ classical casts owned by the Saxon crown by 1785. As even Napoleon discovered, it was hard, before the 1830s, to extract real artifacts from the Ottoman domains. In the course of the first Prussian expedition to Egypt in 1820-25, mostly designed to collect specimens of natural history, nine of the scholars died of illnesses, most of their instruments broke, and the majority of their time was expended waiting for the Bedouin chiefs on whom they depended to negotiate their passage through hostile lands, where the visitors were repeatedly robbed or blackmailed.[30] Not surprisingly, their results were disappointing. Collections of Egyptian artifacts did grow, in Paris, of course, and in Turin, in Britain, and more slowly, in Berlin. After Austen Henry Layard's excavations, Assyrian artifacts began to come westward. But that was only after mid-century; it is worth noting that the general public didn't get a glimpse of the Ishtar Gate in Berlin until 1934! In the United States, the holdings were even more paltry.

To summarize: by the 1830s, Oriental studies was suffering from asymmetrical specialization, a strong whiff of scholarly inferiority, a severe lack of academic positions and patronage, and a paucity of artifacts for study and exhibition. How then to defend the study of the Orient? Now that we can see this as a problem for Salisbury, we can begin to appreciate the ways in which he and his fellow Orientalists tried to solve it. I want to conclude, then, with a brief discussion of the ways in which Oriental studies in the 1830s and 1840s addressed itself to this context and sought to reclaim its relevance and scholarly authority. Falling directly in this era, Salisbury's discourse allows us to see some of the ways in which he, like his fellow Orientalists, tried to make the case for the scholarly, political, and cultural importance of his field.

Writing in a world in which Romanticism lasted longer than was the case in Europe, Salisbury expended considerable effort in convincing his audience of the beauties of Arabic, Persian, and Sanskrit poetry,[31] though he was also well aware that he could claim for it aesthetic status equal to that of classical literature. He writes:

> …I would simply say that the scholar whose taste has been refined by the classics, or even he whose ideal of beauty is embodied in the higher productions of European literature, will still find beauties to admire in the expressions of the cultivated mind of the Arab and the Brahman, though he must, indeed, divest himself of the prepossessions of classic and European association, and enter into the scenery and various relations of the Oriental world,

so far as to be able to recognize the Beautiful in forms and colors peculiar to the East.[32]

This is already faint praise against earlier, stronger Romantic claims to the beauty of Hebrew poetry—made by Herder, for example—or Goethe's devotion to Hafiz. A stronger argument for the importance of Oriental verse can be found, however, in defending Arabic poetry, in particular, as a propadeutic for appreciating the beauties of the Bible. Salisbury quotes a passage written by de Sacy, perhaps thirty years previously:

> If the study of ancient Arabic poetry can assist us, as it doubtless can, in penetrating more deeply into the sanctuary of the poetry of ancient Zion; if with its aid we can dispel any of the obscurity which renders us less sensible to the sublime poetry of Isaiah, to the eloquent lamentations of Jeremiah, to the bold and fearful pictures of Ezekiel, to the bitter mournings and the vivid expressions of conscious innocence of Job....can we regret the labor we have devoted to acquiring a knowledge from which we reap such results?[33]

In 1843, on the continent, this would have seemed a terribly amateurish means of defending the study of Oriental languages, but evidently Salisbury thought it still had the power to touch Romantic American hearts.

Much longer lasting as a selling point and far more dangerous is another argument for the Orient's utility Salisbury sketches: that Indo-European linguistics can be used as a means to secure for Oriental studies the right to tell a *deeper* history of the human race or races than can the classicists or the Bible. Begun already by William Jones in the 1780s, and extended by Friedrich Schlegel and Franz Bopp, this linguistic family-tree mapping had the great advantage, for the dawning positivist age, that it converted the study of poetry into something seemingly more 'scientific.' Combined with new forms of nationalism, it also inclined scholars to seek the primeval homelands of 'their' people—conceived in cultural or proto-racial terms. Friedrich Schlegel, in 1808, had already used linguistic tools to begin to reconstruct the westward emigration of the *Germanen*, whose relationship to the Indians, Persians, and Greeks marked them as carriers of a higher culture (and more flexible tongues and minds) than the peoples descended from other language groups. In 1820, in an extremely lengthy discussion of the *Shahnameh*, Joseph Hammer—an anti-clerical mason and from Metternich's point of view a dangerous liberal—made the further claim that Sanskrit poetry and the Zend Avesta were far older than Hebrew 'documents.' One of the earliest essays to use linguistic relationships to pinpoint an 'Aryan' [34] homeland, Hammer's review argued that 'Arieme,' in eastern Iran, not Ur (home of Abraham) was the seat of the oldest culture.[35] By the mid-1820s, thanks to Hammer and others,[36] the terms for the language groups Schlegel had sketched were already settling into 'Aryan' and 'Semite,' in part so that specialists in these linguistic groups could write histories rooted in the first religious and poetic texts of these people. Their aim was not, however, to *divide* East and West, but as was clearly the case for Max Müller and for most Jewish and Christian Hebrew Bible scholars, for example, to *link* eastern and western histories, and often to underscore the West's debts to the East.[37]

By the time he came to Europe, Salisbury would have found these early ethno-linguistic diffusionary histories in many of the scholarly works he read, and they clearly left their traces on his thinking. Let us listen to Salisbury make the case for the importance of studying Sanskrit *poetry* for the purposes of history: "…the uncertainty as yet of all but a few of the traditional dates of Indian history, and the entire absence of historical annals in Sanskrit, excepting a single work on Cashmir," he argues, "throw us back on the intrinsic peculiarities and internal relations of the literary monuments as the chief source of inference respecting historical events." Literary monuments now have to tell the story of ethnic diffusion, or who had which god first. In fact, they can open up all sorts of unknown histories, Salisbury argues:

> With the touchstone of the Sanskrit, one may discover in a rude, isolated tribe on the Baltic, close affinity to the Arya-race of India; he may hear from the lips of the Irish bard accents which recall an Indian home; he may dispel the mystery of the Gipsy, by tracing him, also, to his origin in one of the low Hindoo casts. By the same test all the Teutonic races are discovered to have intimate family relations with India, while the demonstrated parentage of the languages of classic Greece and Rome from the Sanskrit connects classic antiquity, too, with the Indian. The wide differences of language which appear on a comparison of the oldest form of the Shemitish family, as it may be gathered out of the Hebrew, Arabic, and other dialects, with the Sanskrit, as the most ancient in existence of its own family, are hints of a primeval disruption and alienation between two great branches of the human race, of the reality or manner of which no other record exists.[38]

This is what Bernal misses: there were actually *two* Aryan Models that offered themselves as replacements for the Ancient Model in the Restoration era: the first was the 'Greek miracle' model pushed by the classicists; the second was a model of diffusionary Aryan history, elaborated chiefly by the Sanskritists, one that would later acquire more and more racialized aspects. Neither—*pace* Edward Said—was the product of imperialism, at least in any direct way.

Both, instead, were produced by specialization and competition for cultural capital and the desire to make one's field scientific. If we take this claim seriously, it should be far scarier to us than Bernal's analysis, but it will not indict Orientalists alone. Perhaps had classicists—and biblical scholars—been willing to accept the importance of Oriental studies in its own terms it would not have been inspired to resort to the fateful 'race card' to remind Westerners of their many ties to the East.

There is one last, brief but fascinating appeal to relevance that Salisbury makes at the end of his discourse. He argues that the sultan's failures to secularize—he is witnessing the travails of the Tanzimat reforms in the Ottoman Empire—is a sign of Islam's strength, not weakness. Islam as a religion does *not* need the sword to sustain it, and, he maintains, instead will endure and eventually conflict with Christianity "with other armor and more intensely, than when it struck its scimitars upon the helmeted and mailed champions of the crusades. Are we ready for this encounter?" he asks, suggesting that the West's ignorance of Islam as a popular religion and failure to appreciate the enduring appeal of Islam will be its downfall.[39] Nearly 175 years later, it seems, this lonely Orientalist, trying to explain the importance of his subject in a positivist, classicizing world, already had a good case for Orientalist relevance in ours.

NOTES

1. Edward E. Salisbury, *An Inaugural Discourse on Arabic and Sanskrit Literature, delivered in New Haven, on Wednesday, August 16, 1843* (New Haven: B. L. Hamlen, 1843), 50.

2. Ibid. 11, 35.

3. Ibid. 55.

4. Raymond Schwab's *The Oriental Renaissance: Europe's Rediscovery of India and the East, 1680–1880* (New York: Columbia University Press, 1984), made the case that this Renaissance begins in the later seventeenth century. While I agree in part with this position (one can certainly find sixteenth-century preludes), it is also crucial that we identify the 1820s and 30s as a period of changes so great (including the decipherment of hieroglyphs) as to justify identifying that era as the culmination of a first Renaissance; a second Oriental Renaissance, I have argued elsewhere, begins in the 1870s and 80s. See Marchand, *German Orientalism in the Age of Empire: Religion, Race, and Scholarship* (New York: Cambridge University Press, 2009), 157-211.

5. Martin Bernal, *Black Athena: The Afroasiatic Roots of Classical Civilization,* vol. 1: *The Fabrication of Ancient Greece, 1785-1985* (New Brunswick: Rutgers University Press, 1987), 281-336.

6. On these battles, see Urs App, *The Birth of Orientalism* (Philadelphia: University of

Pennsylvania Press, 2010).

7. Thomas Trautmann, *Aryans and British India* (Berkeley: University of California Press, 1997), 32-35. Ironically, Jomard would also claim that the Egyptian expedition, though virtually without philological assistance, had made "a mockery of everything published about Egypt up to now." Jomard quoted in Fernand Beaucour et al., *The Discovery of Egypt* (Paris: Flammarion, 1990), 200.

8. James Darmesteter, in the introduction to his Avesta translation, says about Jones's critique: "In fact, the only thing in which Jones succeeded was to prove in a decisive manner that the ancient Persians were not equal to the lumières of the eighteenth century, and that the authors of the Avesta had not read the Encyclopédie." Darmesteter, "Introduction," *The Zend Avesta*, Part 1: *The Vendidad, Sacred Books of the East*, vol. IV, ed. F. Max Müller (Oxford: Clarendon Press, 1988), xvi.

9. Herder, *Ideen zur Philosophie der Geschichte der Menschheit*, in *Herders Sämmtliche Werke* 14: 90.

10. I have written about this subject extensively, so will not offer additional detail here; see, e.g., Marchand, "La cassure du continent humaniste: une histoire géologique de la philologie allemande," in *La Philologie allemande, figures de pensée, Revue Germanique Internationale* 14 (2011): 225-37.

11. By the 1820s, he was one of the most severe and incisive critics of Jomard and other Romantic era scholars. Jed Z. Buchwald and Diane Greco Josefowicz, *The Zodiac of Paris: How an Improbable Controversy over an Ancient Egyptian Artifact Provoked a Modern Debate Between Religion and Science* (Princeton: Princeton University Press, 2010), 327.

12. Christian Lassen, *Die Altpersischen Keilinschriften von Persepolis* (Bonn: Eduard Weber, 1836), 182.

13. Marchand, *German Orientalism*, 83.

14. "In Memoriam," in *Journal of the American Oriental Society* 22 (1901): 1-6.

15. On Newton's chronology, see, mostly recently, Jed Z. Buchwald and Mordechai Feingold, *Newton and the Origins of Civilization* (Princeton: Princeton University Press, 2013).

16. Buchwald and Josefowicz, *Zodiac of Paris*, 164.

17. On the Creuzer Streit, see George Williamson, *The Longing for Myth in Germany: Religion and Aesthetic Culture from Romanticism to Nietzsche* (Chicago: University of Chicago Press, 2004), 137-50; Josine Blok, "Quests for a Scientific Mythology: F. Creuzer and K. O. Müller on History and Myth," in *History and Theory* 33:4 (1994): 26-52; and Marchand, *German Orientalism*, 66-74.

18. On Creuzer's methods, see Eva Kocziszky, "Samothrake: Ein Streit um Creuzers Symbolik und das Wesen der Mythologie," in *Antike und Abendland* 43 (1997): 174-89, and Blok, "Quests for a Scientific Mythology."

19. Voss's two-volume *Antisymbolik* (1824-26) recycled and extended criticisms of Creuzer he had made in earlier essays. On Voss, see Wilhelm Herbst, *Johann Heinrich Voss*, vol. 2, pt. 2 (Leipzig: B. G. Teubner, 1876), 106-220.

20. J. G. Rhode, *Die Heilige Sage und das gesammte Religionssystem der alten Baktrer, Meder*

und Perser oder des Zendvolks (Frankfurt am Main: Hermannsche Buchhandlung, 1820), v-ix, 12.

21. *Prolegomena to a Scientific System of Mythology,* [1825] transl. John Leitch (London: Longman, Brown, Green, and Longmans, 1845), 37; 268-73; 318-23.

22. The now-forgotten Romantic theologian Augustus Tholuck translated mystical Islamic poetry from Persian, Turkish, and Arabic collections in the Royal Library in Berlin in 1818-19 because, he claimed: "Familiarity with it is important for the history of philosophy and religion, poetry is thereby greatly enriched, and throughout the deep religious content of most passages is closely related to the spirit of our present age." Tholuck noted the similarity of religious feeling between believers, even without a common biblical core. Tholuck, *Blüthensammlung aus der Morgenländischen Mystik* (Berlin: Ferdinand Dämmler, 1825), ii.

23. Friedrich Max Müller, *India: What Can it Teach Us?* (London: Longmans, 2nd ed. 1892), 33.

24. A. W. Schlegel to Christian Lassen, 28 Nov. 1825, in *Briefwechsel A. W. von Schlegel/ Christian Lassen*, ed. W. Kirfel (Bonn: Verlag Friedrich Cohen, 1914), 170.

25. Marchand, *German Orientalism*, 96.

26. Lassen to Schlegel, 11 Jan 1824, in *Briefwechsel*, 17. On scholarly conditions in France, see Schlegel to Lassen, Sept. 1824, and Lassen to Schlegel, 2 July 1825, in ibid., 68-8; 138.

27. Marchand, *German Orientalism*, 95-101.

28. Marchand, *German Orientalism*, 77.

29. Ed Weech and Nancy Charley, "After the Fashion of their Country," *Times Literary Supplement,* 29 April 2016, 14-15.

30. C. G. Ehrenberg, ed., *Naturgeschichtliche Reisen durch Nord-Afrika und West-Asien in den Jahren 1820 bis 1825 on Dr. W. F. Hemprich und Dr. C. G. Ehrenberg,* vol. 1 (Berlin: Ernst Siegfried Mittler, 1828).

31. E.g. Salisbury, *Inaugural Discourse*, 29, 34.

32. Ibid. 42.

33. Ibid. 43-44.

34. In the 1770s, this category seems to have been used by two separate groups, geographically inclined historians trying to tease out of Tacitus a history of the German tribes and scholars of ancient Persia ('Aria'). For the former, see, e.g., Johann Christoph Gatterer, *Einleitung in die synchronistische Universalhistorie*, vol. 2 (1771), 820. The key to uniting them and driving the common homeland back to India or eastern Iran seems to have been the linguistic association of the Sanskrit 'Arya' with the ancient Persian term for their country, 'Aria,' and Herodotus' remark, at 7.62 that long ago everyone had called the Medes 'Arians.' The Sanskrit and Avestan texts—in which 'Arya' or 'Aria' occurred frequently—worked as a confirmation of Herodotus, and Jones's etymological link to the Germans permitted the mixing of Tacitus's laudatory characterizations of the *Germanen* with praise for the noble people in the vedas.

35. Joseph Hammer, "Schahnameh" (reviewing Joseph Goerres's translation) in A. W. Schlegel's Viennese *Jahrbücher der Literatur* 1820 vol. 9, 7-83 and vol. 10, 210-56; here 24, 36, 40.

36. Hammer's is the earliest use of the term in this sense that I know of. Many of the recent commentators on 'Aryanism' are very vague about when exactly the term came into use. This is true of Trautmann, of Stefan Arvidsson (*Aryan Idols: Indo-European Mythology as Ideology and Science,* transl. Sonia Wichmann [Chicago: University of Chicago Press, 2006]); of Maurice Olender (*The Languages of Paradise: Race, Religion and Philology in the Nineteenth Century*, trans. Arthur Goldhammer [Cambridge, Mass.: Harvard University Press, 1992]); and of Christopher Krebs (*A Most Dangerous Book: Tacitus's Germania from the Roman Empire to the Third Reich* [New York: W. W. Norton, 2012]). Tuska Benes, in her regrettably often overlooked *In Babel's Shadow: Language, Philology and the Nation in Nineteenth-Century Germany* [Detroit: Wayne State University Press, 2008], 202) notes the importance of Julius Klaproth in popularizing the term; but closer investigation is warranted on this point.

37. See, e.g., the extended discussions in Trautmann, *Aryans and British India*; and Susannah Heschel, *Abraham Geiger and the Jewish Jesus* (Chicago: University of Chicago Press, 1997); and Marchand, *German Orientalism,* of the ways in which these linkages were formed, of course often with condescending, supercessionalist, or even imperial presumptions with respect to the Orient guiding them. This does not mean, however, that the Orientalists always cast the 'Orient' as other; it was, to the contrary, strongly bound up with Western history.

38. Salisbury, *Inaugural Discourse*, 34.

39. Ibid. 54.

Edward Salisbury and
A. I. Silvestre de Sacy

Benjamin R. Foster

The year is 1837. With the magic powers of authorship, I spare our elegant young Yankee couple, Edward and Abigail Salisbury, as well as their two servants, an interminable, bone-jarring trip across France by stagecoach, while we approach Paris by air and admire six imposing monuments dominating its Orientalist landscape.

The first is the output of a profession that had first appeared in Europe 250 years before, that is, the Christian professor of Hebrew. Already by 1550, there were at least thirteen such, mostly in Germany, and by 1830 they were everywhere. The incumbents lectured on the Hebrew Bible, taught the language, and published biblical commentaries, Hebrew grammars, and dictionaries in profusion; some 3000 Hebrew titles were printed in Europe before 1600 alone. Hebrew had joined Latin and Greek as a language of Christian humanist scholarship.[1]

Young Salisbury would have known something about this. He would have known the names, at least, of some of the leading German Hebraists, from the elder Buxtorf to Gesenius.[2] He surely knew that Noah Webster insisted that English was a direct descendant of Aramaic, if only because his own teacher, Josiah Gibbs, had provided Webster with his Semitic etymologies.[3] Americans were also basking in the warm sunlight of von Herder's romantic lucubrations on Hebrew poetry, which had just been translated into English and printed in 1833.[4] I expect young Salisbury had delved into it.

The monument of a second, younger, profession looms on the landscape as well, the Christian professor of Arabic, an innovation of the early seventeenth century, but this one concentrated in northern Europe: Holland and England.[5] Arabic study was largely free of the Scriptural angst of biblical Hebrew, but had anxieties of its own, mostly concealed by the fact that very few European Orientalists had any real competence in that language. Here at Yale, Ezra Stiles had tried his hand at Arabic, and his arch enemy and successor Timothy Dwight was also said to have studied Arabic.[6] But the fact is that when the diplomats from the Barbary States arrived to negotiate with Jefferson, no one in the United States could read their credentials, a nice forerunner to the regular ritual laments in our culture that Americans don't know strategic foreign languages. Jefferson owned an English translation of the Koran, but I wonder if he ever read it.[7]

Our third monument as we approach Paris: Salisbury would have known of the exciting European discoveries of Eastern Christians and the peoples of other sects —Copts, Maronites, Jacobites, Armenians, Ethiopians, Samaritans —and their languages. Ethiopic, for example, had appeared on the European horizon in 1513,[8] Syriac in 1539.[9] Coptic had been a hot topic in the seventeenth-century Republic of Letters as a possible key to ancient Egyptian hieroglyphs.[10] One of Champollion's first publications was on Samaritan.[11] Orientalists were supposed to know all the languages of the Orient and more were turning up all the time.

By the end of the seventeenth century, with the desacralization of Hebrew, came the handbooks of Semitic languages, our fourth monument. An example that reached the New World was Christian Ravis's *General Grammar for the ready attaining of the Hebrew, Samaritan, Chaldee, Syriac, Arabic, and Ethiopic languages* (1650). Fixated on roots, as was the fashion in an age when etymology reigned as the queen of the linguistic sciences, Ravis calculated 8000 possibilities of triconsonantal roots in Hebrew, though the Dutch Arabist Schultens later upstaged him with 12,000 possible roots, of which only 2000 survived in the Bible, yielding a staggering potential Semitic vocabulary of 300,000 words.[12] So, a century and half before Salisbury landed in France, Oriental languages were much in the air and copies of key publications had made their way to the libraries of Yale and Harvard. According to these handbooks, Oriental languages were easy to learn. Brian Walton, in his 1655 *Introductio ad Lectionem Linguarum Orientalium*, had opined that you could learn Arabic in five weeks of assiduous study, but our hero Salisbury would soon know better than that.[13]

Oriental polyglottism had, moreover, found its apogee in our fifth monument: brobdingnagian multilingual publishing projects that the invention of movable type had made possible for the first time in human civilization, though no computer could do them today: I mean, of course, the huge polyglot Bibles of Alcalá (Complutens, 1520), Antwerp (1571–80), and Paris (1629–57), all under the auspices of the Catholic church, and finally London (1654–71), the first book in history published by public subscription, the last in six massive volumes with the biblical text in nine languages plus independent Latin translations of each of the versions.[14]

We may also mention as our sixth monument the first Oriental translation project, on the threshold of the Enlightenment, D'Herbelot's *Bibliothèque Orientale* of 1697.[15] This was a mine of information for historians such as Edward Gibbon, who did not want to study a lot of languages, in his case not even Greek.

All this was intimidating. Salisbury would have had a taste of it from his mentor, Josiah Gibbs, remembered affectionately as the most boring teacher on the Yale faculty.[16] But Salisbury was a modern young man with a modern agenda. Some of our monuments are old stuff. We can trace Orientalist study of Hebrew and Aramaic to late antiquity, of Arabic at least to the tenth century. If Hebrew focused on the Bible, Arabic had gone through various stages. To Salisbury, the appeal of Arabic would no longer be Averroism, optics, conic sections, medicine, advice on how to rule, or natural history, but belles-lettres. There were no copies of Arabic belletristic works in the United States and no one who could have read them if there had been. They had not even been printed, for the most part, but were available only in prized manuscript collections jealously guarded by their owners. Arabic literature was certainly one goal our hero intended to pursue.[17]

But what was really new was what Raymond Schwab termed the second Renaissance of Europe, or the "Oriental Renaissance," in which Persian and Sanskrit had an impact on European thought in the late eighteenth and early nineteenth centuries no less important than the impact of Classical and Patristic Greek and Latin on European thought in the earlier Renaissance.[18] A new horizon has opened up. The narrow Mediterranean world has expanded so that Franz Bopp's Berlin now links to Iran and India, and the Semitic peoples have been left isolated in a narrow steppe and desert zone in Western Asia, hemmed in by the Indo-Iranian grassland peoples shortly to be invented, largely on the basis of the *Shah-name*.[19]

The first American to see the importance of this new development was Yale's Ezra Stiles, who had been fascinated by the anniversary discourses of Sir William Jones on Persian and Sanskrit.[20] Stiles had even written Oriental Jones, as he was called, a 130-page letter, which, alas, arrived in India only after Jones's untimely death.[21]

Jones had promoted both Persian and Sanskrit in the outgoing eighteenth century. A generation or two before Jones, the Persian narrative in Europe had been based on Herodotus and Xenophon. Herodotus held up the Achaemenid kings as examples of Oriental tyranny defeated by the valiant Greeks, whereas Xenophon held up Cyrus as a model of the enlightened despot.[22] Xenophon's Persia had already been welcome news to Europeans of the sixteenth century who saw, from afar, Safavid Iran as a noble rival to the nearer Ottoman Empire they knew and feared, though to the Catholic missionaries and the agents of the East India Country on the ground, the Safavid court seemed like Oriental despotism at its most capricious and frightening.[23] True, the Persians were mentioned in Classical sources and the Bible, so at least had a place in the civilized world, but not the Turks, unless they were Gog and Magog.[24]

On the other hand, Persian literary tradition, as exemplified by the *Shah-name* or what little was known of Sassanian culture, had never heard of the Achaemenid kings. Even at Persepolis their names were utterly forgotten. Jones had popularized Persian poetry to the extent that a reading knowledge of Classical Persian was an accomplishment worthy of a liberal-minded English gentleman.[25] Salisbury, however, if he had not avoided looking at Jones's books, surely saw Hafiz as soft porn. For this fastidious Yankee, who wrote that you should not use red and blue in your home-decorating scheme because they were jarringly Oriental, cups of wine, ardent damsels, and beautiful boys were not to be countenanced.[26] But Salisbury was just in time to learn about Old Persian, which was rather different fare, and linked wonderfully with Herodotus.[27] So, two Persias to choose from: an Indo-European one and a Herodotean one, and Salisbury chose the latter.

Sanskrit, for its part, stood at the roots of the newly invented Indo-European culture, and the *Institutes of Manu* were chaste and serious reading compared to the effusions of the Persian libertines. Salisbury was brave to take up both Arabic and Sanskrit at once, when, with his money and appreciation for the arts, he could have found many other pursuits in Paris worthy of his time; he was thrilled at Berlin in 1838, for example, by a performance of a Bach Passion, perhaps conducted by Mendelssohn himself.

American knowledge of Hebrew was at least a century behind European standards. A few Americans could perhaps read a few words of Arabic and Syriac, while the other languages of the Christian Orient, not to mention Old Persian, Avestan, and Sanskrit, were entirely unknown.

One man dominated this new, what we might justifiably call, Empire of Letters. He was A. I. Silvestre de Sacy, Europe's premier Orientalist, a royalist who had survived the Revolution and accepted a teaching post from the new government until such time as a suitable republican candidate could replace him, which, needless to say, did not occur.[28] Who else would Goethe dedicate a book to, calling him "Unser Meister"? Who else would Carsten Niebuhr correspond with at length concerning his discoveries in Iran, giving rise to de Sacy's path-breaking study of Pahlavi, along with a treatise on Sassanian coinage? Or, who else would Europe's leading biblical scholar, Eichhorn, praise for his translation of Samaritan letters, and correspond with assiduously when it was possible politically? Who else would have a private audience with Pope Pius VII, during which he addressed the pontiff in well-turned Latin? De Sacy was the man whom Napoleon would ask, "Comment va l'Arabe?" —How's the Arabic going?—the same man of whom the young Egyptian reformer Tahtawi wrote that even if his spoken Arabic was halting and his written Arabic not idiomatic, his knowledge of Arabic language and literature was astonishing, even though he had never set foot in the Arab world.[29]

Our *mise-en-scène* is the small but remarkable scholarly community centered around the Collège de France, which, like de Sacy himself, had miraculously survived the Revolution, and, even more miraculously, survived Napoleon, who nursed imperial visions of what it should be teaching.[30] The students in the 1795 Oriental Institute of Paris, or École des Langues Orientales, now called by its alums "Langues'O,"[31] were subject to the draft just as they were making progress: young Champollion, for example, was ordered out of class to go to Iran as a consul, where he could have wasted the rest of his career in petty diplomatic intrigue instead of deciphering Egyptian, but managed to get out of it by family influence.[32] So much for our cast of characters and our setting. Now for some interaction.

I wish we knew more of the reaction of the senior Orientalist scholar of Europe to a rich, serious young American who wanted to learn Arabic and had probably never spoken much French in his life. Is it possible that de Sacy had never even met an American before? Years later, Salisbury remembered him as a "truly saintly Jansenist in spirit, [who] won all hearts by his perfect learning communicated with the greatest mildness."[33] I like to think that the ascetic, Calvinist, even Judaizing aspects of Jansenism, not to mention its durability among influential circles of the Paris *haute bourgeoisie*, resonated on a personal level to a New England Congregationalist in a way orthodox Catholicism never could.[34]

De Sacy's teaching style might well have appealed to Salisbury's New England sense of practicality. De Sacy was a proponent of what is now known as "Porte Royale" grammar, according to which there are universal grammatical categories one can apply to any language, anathema to modern linguists, who like to celebrate diversity.[35] De Sacy's succinct little treatise for young people on the practical value of universal grammar for learning languages had been translated into English and printed at Moses Stuart's press at Andover, Massachusetts, in 1834.[36] Of course Salisbury owned a copy.

But de Sacy was also the first Christian Arabist to make an effort to understand the hair-splitting treatises of the Arab grammarians and what we now refer to as "native grammatical categories"—and, moreover, to go beyond their letter to their spirit, trying to understand what these writers saw themselves as doing.[37] De Sacy's own massive Arabic grammar, which he published as a requirement for his job, was the first usable Arabic grammar published in Europe.[38] He also did some lighter projects, like translating fables and an Arabic treatise on the carrier pigeon, which he saw as a miracle of speedy communication in that pre-telegraph age.[39]

Among his many interests, de Sacy was a proponent of Arabic belles-lettres, that is, works that educated Arabs professed to admire, at least out of a sense of duty, such as the Pre-Islamic odes and the euphuistic *Maqamat* of al-Hariri, of which de Sacy himself published a critical edition.[40] The only way to read Arabic literature was to find manuscripts, of which de Sacy had one of the richest collections in Europe. The only way to understand Arabic literature was to own real Arabic dictionaries, not European works like Golius, with their one-word Latin entries, helpful as they might be, but multi-volume Arabic works available only in manuscript, prolix and complicated, the consultation of which requires a superior knowledge of Arabic just to look up a word. De Sacy likewise produced the most important anthology of Arabic literature for language study in nineteenth-century Europe, offering richer reading than such dreary homework of his predecessors as Ibn Arabshah's metrical life of Tamerlane.[41]

Another of de Sacy's students recorded his first impression of the man: small, hunched, dare one say homely by the standards of arrogant youth, but with wonderfully bright, piercing eyes.[42] His own regime of lectures, classes, meetings, administrative, and political work I would find utterly over-whelming. The man was everywhere, involved in everything, or what we would now call the "go-to" person for anything to do with the Orient, near or far.[43]

For the serious student, the libraries of Paris were unrivalled; indeed French agents had followed Napoleon's armies and picked out for France the rarest books and choicest manuscripts in the collections of Germany and Italy.[44] There was even an Arab community in Paris, largely Egyptian expatriots who had collaborated with the French occupation of Egypt and found it expedient to withdraw with the French military.[45]

In an age of books, de Sacy had them all in his study. Salisbury attended the auction of his library after his death, in over 6000 lots, and the modern scholar peruses his holdings with awe.[46] De Sacy owned, for example, the most important Christian printed Bibles, including the Complutensian, Antwerp, Paris, and London Polyglots, not to mention the best Jewish Bibles as well. Our first and fifth monuments sat together on his bookshelves. As for our second and fourth monuments, he owned virtually every European, Egyptian, Ottoman and Indian printed book in Arabic, Persian, Syriac, Ethiopic, Samaritan, and Turkish, for Arabic beginning with the Fano prayer book of 1531,[47] including even a Lebanese Arabic psalter printed in Bucharest in 1747. The Oriental Renaissance? He owned every title and they tended to fetch the highest prices. His too was a breathtaking collection of grammars of every Semitic language, including such rarities as the so-called Arabic grammars of Pedro de Alcalá and Postel, plus hundreds of books on travel and exploration (including, for instance, a full set of the Napoleonic *Description de l'Égypte*), volumes on religion, Classical languages and history, periodicals, offprints, catalogues, biographies, collected works, in short, a working and rare-book library beyond compare. And this was just the left-overs after the choicest part of his collection went to the Bibliothèque Nationale. Thanks to Salisbury, some of these treasures repose today on the shelves of Yale's Sterling Memorial Library.

Hard for us to understand today are two aspects of the world of study that confronted Salisbury. First, its essential unity, seen from the outside: there was no concept of ancient, medieval, or modern, and no sense of specialization. The world from Constantinople to Bombay was one universe of exciting new discoveries, competition, sharing, and trophy-gathering. I offer for comparison the space race as we saw it in the 1960s—there were no specialists in the moon or Jupiter or asteroids but the whole of space beyond planet Earth was seen as one agenda where likewise there was exploration, competition, and trophy-gathering.

Now for the ancient Near East. Anthony Grafton once asked himself when Europe first developed a sense of the ancient Near East as a separate field of study from the Orient *grosso modo*. His answer was Joseph Scaliger's defense, about 1602, of the authenticity of certain fragments of Berossos preserved in such ancient authors as Clement of Alexandria, George Syncellus, and Josephus. Scaliger was thus willing to accept as an authentic relic of the past

Berossos's not exactly biblical story of the creature Oannes coming out of the sea and teaching men the arts of civilization. Although Scaliger thought such things were mere fables, he argued that they should be preserved for their own sake out of proper reverence for antiquity. "He thus offered the modern world its first genuine large-scale products of the ancient Near East, works so alien to the Western tradition that they could hardly be interpreted at all until the discovery of parallel records in cuneiform, more than two hundred years later."[48] The Assyriologists among us might quibble with Grafton's statement, insofar as much of the material in Berossos is still problematic when compared to cuneiform sources.[49] But what matters here is that to Salisbury and his generation, the Orient was so broad and exciting, that, like outer space in our own time, it seemed almost impossible to grasp, but, at the same time, a sublime unity.

In France of the mid-nineteenth-century, the rhetoric was, obviously, different. The Orient was then described as a world both Old and New—the Old World as the cradle of civilization, the New World as a place of exploration and discovery.[50] The magic key to both these worlds was no longer voyages, however, but language study. Here I will let de Sacy speak for himself:

> The more remote the nations we study are from the narrow circle in which we live, in time and space, manners, customs, and beliefs, the more striking and multifarious the contrasts they offer us, the more so, as we come to know them, …. do we feel ourselves caught up in mounting interest and irresistible attraction. Perhaps it is just this hidden relationship that, almost without their knowing it, draws even ordinary people towards distant lands and long-forgotten peoples. Nevertheless, such a study can bear no real fruit for anyone who has not readied himself through long and arduous preparation. There are two principal means to attaining this end, travel and language study. Of these two, the former is of very little use without the latter. Knowledge of languages can, on the other hand, dispense with the fatigues of travel, for it husbands the all too short time we are given to live, not to mention the physical strength so necessary to exercise our moral faculties. It has the further advantage of making distance of time and place disappear. One may add that languages bear within themselves one of the most characteristic traits of nations and that a people's level of civilization, their beliefs, and the inclinations of their moral and intellectual faculties are heavily influenced by their language; these are indiscernible only to those whose lack of reflection has left them insensible to what languages so luminously betoken.[51]

For many Orientalists of the 1840s and 1850s, the portal to the Old World and the New, both in time and place, was Persia, and so, back in New Haven, Salisbury's first article was on Old Persian, just as de Sacy's first major publication had been on Pahlavi and Sassanian Iran.[52] Iranian studies, as we now call them, provided the essential context for the decipherment of cuneiform. I take this occasion to applaud Salisbury for buying a copy of the first grammar of Akkadian, published by Jules Oppert, who forsook mathematics to study Old Persian with Christian Lassen and who became Europe's first Professor of Assyriology, appointed in Paris naturally, where else?[53] In a scholarly world before transliteration had been invented, the verb paradigms were there printed using the Hebrew alphabet. So too Salisbury bought a copy of Layard's folio *Monuments of Nineveh,* and not just the best-selling parlor-table octavo narrative of Layard's adventures, which the aged English poet Wordsworth once pronounced the most interesting modern book he had read.[54]

In due course our fellow traveler, Edward Salisbury, looking out at the awe-inspiring constellations in the Orientalist sky as he knew it, felt understandably humbled, even inadequate, for the growing demands of mid-nineteenth-century specialist scholarship.[55] Yet, he was present at creation, and had done his best to transport the Orientalist world of Paris, not only its Société and *Journal Asiatique,* but its values and its books and manuscripts as well, to New Haven, to an empty classroom, a tiny library by Paris standards, and to a minuscule readership. The transplant was slow to flourish and, perforce, drew its continued inspiration from Germany, rather than from Paris, where no figure like de Sacy rose up to succeed him until Ernest Renan, a far more controversial personality and no teacher. Salisbury's successor, William Dwight Whitney, studied Sanskrit at Berlin, not Paris, and was not interested in Arabic (revived at Yale only in 1900 by the appointment of Charles C. Torrey). But, looking back, we see Salisbury as the right person at the right place at the right time. I think he knew that, even if he soon wanted to lay the burden down.[56] The small-town culture of mid-nineteenth-century American college faculty life must have made his academic adventures in Paris, Bonn, and Berlin seem, like the ancient Orient itself, far away indeed in both time and space.

NOTES

1. Useful introductions to various aspects of the history of the Christian study of Hebrew touched on here include Jerome Friedman, *The Most Ancient Testimony: Sixteenth-Century Christian-Hebraica in the Age of Renaissance Nostalgia* (Athens, Ohio: University

of Ohio Press, 1983); Karl Burmeister, *Sebastian Münster: Versuch eines biographischen Gesamtbildes, Basler Beiträge zur Geschichtswissenschaft* 91 (Basel: Helbing & Lichtenhahn, 1969); Alexandre Lorian, "L'imprimerie hébraïque 1470–1550: ateliers chrétiens et ateliers juifs," in *Le livre dans l'Europe de la Renaissance, Actes du XXVIIIᵉ Colloque Humaniste de Tours,* ed. Pierre Aquilon and Henri-Jean Martin (Paris: Promodis, 1988), 219–29; Marie-Louise Demonet-Lannay, "La désacralisation de l'hébreu au XVIᵉ siècle," in *L'Hébreu au temps de la Renaissance,* ed. Ilana Zinguer (Leiden: Brill, 1992), 154–71; Percy S. Allen, "The Trilingual Colleges of the Early Sixteenth Century," in *Erasmus: Lectures and Wayfaring Sketches* (Oxford: Clarendon, 1934), 138–63. For a broad survey of the subject, Abraham Melamed, "The Revival of Christian Hebraism in Early Modern Europe," in *Philosemitism in History,* ed. Jonathan Karpe and Adam Sutcliffe (Cambridge: Cambridge University Press, 2011), 49–66.

2. For Buxtorf, Stephen G. Burnett, *From Christian Hebraism to Jewish Studies: Johannes Buxtorf (1564–1629) and Hebrew Learning in the Seventeenth Century* (Leiden: Brill, 1996); Wilhelm Gesenius was well known in the United States through the Hebrew grammar of Moses Stuart (1821), based on Gesenius's Hebrew grammar, and the translations of his Hebrew dictionary by Josiah Gibbs (1828, 1831) and Edward Robinson (1836, who had studied with Gesenius himself). Salisbury probably knew Gesenius's masterful history of Hebrew grammar and lexicography, *Geschichte der hebräischen Sprache und Schrift, eine philologisch-historische Einleitung in die Sprachlehren und Wörterbücher der hebräischen Sprache* (Leipzig: Vogel, 1815).

3. Noah Webster, *Dissertation on the English Language* (1789, numerous printings), revised and expanded in *An American Dictionary of the English Language ... to which is prefixed an Introductory Dissertation on the Origin, History, and Connection, of the Languages of Western Asia and Europe, with an Explanation of the Principles on which Languages are Formed ...* (Springfield, Mass: Merriam, numerous editions). Webster was among the last to link Hebrew with the Indo-European languages through word pairs (*rechus* and riches, *shekel* and skill, *shevah* and seven, *ever* and over, etc.) and alleged expanded monosyllables (tar/ter/tor/tro = "force", hence *taurus* "bull" was related to torrent, target, trunk, trepan, detriment, tardy ...). Gibbs even suggested that English "arc" was derived from Arabic *arikha,* "to emit odor," how semantically is not clear. Semitic etymologies, lavishly printed in the original scripts, remained in Webster's dictionary until 1864, whereas this type of scholarship had largely disappeared in Europe 150 years before. Franklin Edgerton, "Notes on Early American Work in Linguistics," *Proceedings of the American Philosophical Society* 87 (1943): 26, comments, "Even the relative isolation of American scholarship from Europe hardly excuses such astounding ignorance in Webster ..."

4. Johann Gottfried von Herder, *The Spirit of Hebrew Poetry, translated from the German by James Marsh* (Burlington, Vermont: Smith, 1833), originally published in 1782. To von Herder, Hebrew poetry was wonderfully terse and simple, infantile and vivid, close to nature, full of passion, evoking a lost world of herdsmen looking up at a great sky at dawn, singing of the wonder of God's works, and confirming Christian truth.

5. For general introductions to the history of Arabic studies in Europe, Johann Fück,

Die arabischen Studien in Europa bis in den Anfang des 20. Jahrhunderts (Leipzig: Harrassowitz, 1955); Robert Irwin, *For Lust of Knowing: The Orientalists and their Enemies* (London: Penguin, 2006).

6. For Stiles's Arabic notes, Yale University Library Stiles Papers Misc. 502: 1–6 and 166–67, including excerpts from Eutychius of Alexandria.

7. Denise Spellberg, *Thomas Jefferson's Qur'an: Islam and the Founders* (New York: Knopf, 2013), 105–6; for the inability of anyone to read the Arabic credentials, Benjamin R. Foster, "On the Formal Study of Near Eastern Languages in the United States, 1770–1930," in *U.S. – Middle East, Historical Encounters: A Critical Survey,* ed. Abbas Amanat and Magnus T. Bernhardsson (Gainesville: University of Florida Press, 2007), 14, with note 12. Jefferson owned a copy of Sales's treatment of the Koran, by far the most widely circulated in the English-speaking world. Pirated from a little-known book by an Italian Arabist, Sales's work was one of the most successful acts of academic dishonesty in the history of Oriental studies: E. Denison Ross, "Ludovico Marracci," *Bulletin of the School of Oriental and African Studies* 2 (1921): 117–23.

8. Wolf Leslau, *An Annotated Bibliography of the Semitic Languages of Ethiopia* (The Hague: Mouton, 1965); Anna Dorothée von den Brincken, "Johann Potken aus Schwerte, Propst von St. Georg in Köln," in *Aus kölnischer und rheinischer Geschichte: Festgabe Arnold Güttsches zum 65. Geburtstag gewidmet,* ed. Hans Blum (Cologne: Wamper, 1969), 81–114.

9. For a survey of early European publications on Syriac, Andreas G. Hoffmann, *Grammaticae Syriacae* (Halle: Orphanotrophei, 1842); Friedrich Uhlemann, *Grammatik der Syrischen Sprache,* second edition (Berlin: Jonas, 1857), xix–xxii; Werner Strothmann, *Die Anfänge der syrischen Studien in Europa, Göttinger Orientforschungen* 1 (Wiesbaden: Harrassowitz, 1971).

10. Sydney Aufrère, *La momie et la tempête: Nicolas-Claude Fabri de Peiresc et la "Curiosité Egyptienne" en Provence au début du XVIIe siècle* (Avignon: Barthémy, 1990); A. Bresson, "Peiresc et les études coptes: Prolégomènes au déchiffrement des hiéroglyphs," *XVIIe Siècle* 40 (1988): 41–50; Francis W. Gravit, "Peiresc et les études coptes en France au XVIIe siècle," *Bulletin de la société d'archéologie copte* 4 (1938): 1–21.

11. Hermine Hartleben, *Jean-François Champollion: Sa vie et son oeuvre,* translated by Denise Meunier, ed. C. Desroches Noblecourt (Paris: Pygmalion, 1983), 97; James D. Purvis, *The Samaritan Pentateuch and the Origins of the Samaritan Sect, Harvard Semitic Studies* 2 (1968); Robert T. Anderson and Terry Giles, *The Samaritan Pentateuch: An Introduction to its Origin, History, and Significance for Biblical Studies* (Atlanta: Society of Biblical Literature, 2012); *The Samaritans,* ed. Allan D. Crown (Tübingen: Mohr, 1989); Peter N. Miller, "A Philologist, a Traveller and an Antiquary Rediscover the Samaritans in Seventeenth-Century Paris, Rome and Aix: Jean Morin, Pietro della Valle and N.-C. Fabri de Peiresc," in *Die Praktiken der Gelehrsamkeit in der frühen Neuzeit,* ed. Helmut Zedelmaier and Martin Mulsow (Tübingen: Niemeyer, 2001), 123–46.

12. For Ravis, G. J. Toomer, *Eastern Wisedome and Learning* (Oxford: Oxford University Press, 1996); for Schultens, Fück, op. cit. note 5, 105–7.

13. Brian Walton, *In Biblia Polyglotta Prolegomena,* ed. D. A. I. Dathe (Leipzig: Weygand, 1777), 42–43.

14. Henry J. Todd, *Memoirs of the Life and Writings of Right Rev. Brian Walton* (London: Rivington, 1821).

15. Fück, op. cit. note 5, 98; Bertholomé d'Herbelot, *Bibliothèque Orientale, ou dictionnaire universel contenant généralement tout ce qui regarde la connoissance des Peuples de l'Orient, Leurs Histoires et Traditions véritables ou fabuleuses* (Paris: Galland, 1697), republished several times in the eighteenth century.

16. For Gibbs, Benjamin R. Foster, "Gibbs, Josiah Willard," *American National Biography* (Oxford: Oxford University Press, 1999), vol. 8: 919–20.

17. Franklin Edgerton, "A Letter of Salisbury," *Journal of the American Oriental Society* 64 (1944): 58–61. Some sparse and bizarre information about Arabic poetry would have been available in Salisbury's student days in a posthumously published essay on the subject by Johann David Michaelis, *Arabische Grammatik, nebst einer Arabischen Chrestomathie, und Abhandlung von Arabischen Geschmack, sonderlich in der poetischen und historischen Schreibart,* second edition (Göttingen: Victorinus Bossiegel, 1781). As Michaelis saw it, the pre-Islamic Arabs had achieved some level of excellence in poetry, but the seventh of the most accomplished pre-Islamic poets, Labid, began a process of decline. The ruination of Arabic poetry was completed, according to him, by the Koran, which was so amateurish, despite some fine passages, as to have a chilling effect on Arab creativity. Salisbury owned this pretentious book but it did not dampen his ardor. His own remarks on Arabic poetry, *An Inaugural Discourse on Arabic and Sanskrit Literature, delivered in New Haven, Wednesday, August 16, 1843* (New Haven: Hamlen, 1843), 9–11, 28–30 are far better informed, and he concludes, "… the scholar whose taste has been refined by the classics, or even he whose idea of beauty is embodied in the higher productions of European literature, will still find beauties to admire in the expressions of the cultivated mind of the Arab and the Brahmin." If to a modern reader this may sound condescending, in the time and place it was probably heard as a near revolutionary declaration.

18. Raymond Schwab, *The Oriental Renaissance: Europe's Rediscovery of India and the East 1660–1880,* translated by Gene Patterson-Black and Victor Reinking (New York: Columbia University Press, 1984).

19. As William Dwight Whitney wrote, "The time is long past when reverence for the Hebrew Scriptures as the Book of books could carry with it the corollary that the Hebrew tongue was the most perfect and oldest of all known languages, and even the mother of the rest; it is now fully recognized as merely one in a contracted and very peculiar group of sister dialects, crowded together in a corner of Asia and the adjacent parts of Africa, possessing striking excellences, but also marked with striking defects," *Language and the Study of Language: Twelve Lectures on the Principles of Linguistic Science,* sixth edition (New York: Scribners, 1901), 308.

20. Among the many studies of this crucial figure, Garland Cannon, *The Life and Mind of Oriental Jones* (Cambridge: Cambridge University Press, 1990); Michael J. Franklin, *Orientalist Jones: Sir William Jones, Poet, Lawyer, and Linguist 1746–1794* (Oxford:

Oxford University Press, 2011.

21. Yale University Library Ezra Stiles Papers, Misc. 1108, Jones, Sir William, Letter from ES, 18 Jan 1794.

22. The Greek text of the *Cyropaedia,* a historical romance about the youth of Cyrus the Great, was available in Europe after 1516; in general, Robert Drews, *The Greek Accounts of Near Eastern History* (Cambridge: Harvard University Press, 1973).

23. Lawrence Lockhart, "European Contacts with Persia, 1350–1736," in *The Cambridge History of Iran,* ed. Peter Jackson and Lawrence Lockhart (Cambridge: Cambridge University Press, 1986), vol. 6: 373–411.

24. Margaret Meserve, *Empires of Islam in Renaissance Historical Thought* (Cambridge: Harvard University Press, 2008).

25. One may wonder if Salisbury ever read Jones's translations of Persian poetry, or the work of his followers, such as Richardson, Nott, and Hindley, all of whom translated Hafiz. Thomas Law (d. 1834) was perhaps the only English-speaking resident of the United States of his time proficient in classical Persian, but his career was largely centered around the development of Washington, D.C. and his publications dealt with such matters as establishing a national currency. As a Virginia gentleman, married to a granddaughter of Martha Washington, Law had moved in quite different circles from Salisbury: "Law, Thomas," *Dictionary of National Biography* (Oxford: Oxford University Press, 1917), vol. 11: 676–77.

26. Edward E. Salisbury, *Principles of Domestic Taste* (New Haven: Tuttle, Morehouse & Taylor, 1877), 8: "...because our increasing intercourse with the East has made certain combinations of color fashionable, which only oriental limners and looms have as yet succeeded in bringing together without discord, we should not throw shades of blue and green and red together, rashly." One finds no overt reference to European "Orientalist" painting, which Salisbury surely had seen. He felt, however, that the well-appointed American home should contain "no ornaments, no pictures, no marbles, no forms of furniture, which would have started a blush on the face of the Puritan maiden of the olden time ...," so Orientalism as an art form may be included among what he dismissed as "the art-products of corrupted Rome (meretricious in the worst sense)" and "Paris debauchery" (19).

27. For the decipherment of Old Persian cuneiform writing, Sven Pallis, *The Antiquity of Iraq, A Handbook of Assyriology* (Copenhagen: Munksgaard, 1956), 94–123; *Die Welt des Orients: Keilschrift – Grabungen – Gelehrte,* ed. Rykle Borger et al. (Göttingen: Städtisches Museum Göttingen, 1975); Josef Wiesehöfer, "The Survival and Rediscovery of Ancient Iran," in *Ancient Persia* (London: Tauris, 2010), 223–42.

28. Joseph T. Reinaud, *Notice historique et littéraire sur m. le baron Silvestre de Sacy ...* (Paris: Dondey-Dupré, 1838), republished in *Biographie Universelle Ancienne et Moderne Supplément,* vol. 80 (Paris: Michaud, 1847), 241–68; Hartwig Derenbourg, *Silvestre de Sacy (1758–1838)* (Paris: Leroux, 1895); Henri Dehérain, *Silvestre de Sacy, ses contemporains et ses disciples* (Paris: Geuthner, 1938); Henry Laurens, "Silvestre de Sacy en son temps," in *Silvestre de Sacy: le projet européen d'une science orientaliste,* ed. Michel Espagne, Nora Lafi, and Pascale Rabault-Feuerhahn (Paris: Du Cerf, 2014) 11–21,

being the proceedings of a colloquium held in 2010. Derenbourg (12), enumerating the last living students of de Sacy in 1895, overlooked Salisbury, who was, of course, well beyond his scholarly horizon, nor were the organizers of the 2010 colloquium, focused on de Sacy's role as a founder of modern Oriental studies, aware of his American connection, first revived from oblivion in the writer's essay, "Edward E. Salisbury, America's First Arabist," *Al-'Usur al-Wusta* 9/1 (1997): 15–17 and "Salisbury, Edward Elbridge," *American National Biography* (Oxford: Oxford University Press, 1999), vol. 9: 206–8.

29.   For Goethe, Eichhorn, and Niebuhr, Sabine Mangold-Will, "La question de la reception allemande de Silvestre de Sacy jusqu'en 1815," in *Silvestre de Sacy*, op. cit. note 28, 40–60; for Napoleon, Derenbourg, op. cit. note 28, 23; for Pius VII, Dehérain, op. cit. note 28, xi–xii; for Tahtawi, Mohammed Sabri Ad-Dali, "Un regard égyptien sur Silvestre de Sacy," in *Silvestre de Sacy*, op. cit. note 28, 103–14. De Sacy's personal copy of Tahtawi's *Takhlis al-Ibriz fi Talkhis Bariz* (1834), inscribed to him by the author, is now in the Yale University Library. For an English translation, Daniel L. Newman, *An Imam in Paris: Account of a Stay in France by an Egyptian Cleric (1826–1831)* (London: Saqi, 2004). Hermine Hartleben, biographer of Champollion, sums up de Sacy's position in Paris: "… [his] great personality then stood out so nobly above the seething surface of Paris life, increasingly roiled by fierce partisan enmity, that all sides rendered unreserved homage to him. This man, … deeply deploring the fall of the monarchy, had so utterly immersed himself in his scholarly undertakings and learned to maintain such an unshakeable reserve that even the maelstrom of the Terror had respected his peaceful study [in fact, de Sacy weathered the Terror in the Oise countryside, walking to Paris dressed as a peasant, BRF], and he remained proof against all political and social upheavals …," *Champollion, sein Leben und sein Werk* (Berlin: Weidmann, 1906), vol. 1: 72–73. The French translation and abridgement of this work (above, note 11) being more accessible, I have preferred to cite it here where possible.

30.   For Napoleon and the Collège de France, Abel Lefranc, *Histoire du Collège de France, depuis ses origins jusqu'à la fin du premier Empire* ([1893] reprint: Geneva: Slatkin, 1976), 310–12.

31.   *Deux siècles de l'École des Langues Orientales, Langues'O 1795–1995*, ed. Pierre Labrousse (Paris: Hervas, 1995); this was one of five new schools created by the revolutionary government, and was intended primarily to serve as a training center for diplomatic and commercial interpreters. De Sacy did not speak Arabic, but even in modern times a solid grounding in the Classical form of the language has been deemed a good foundation for subsequent in-country mastery of a spoken dialect, and for commercial purposes spoken Italian was probably more useful anyway.

32.   Hartleben, *Champollion,* op. cit. note 11, 88.

33.   Edgerton, op. cit. note 17, 60. Salisbury took mostly private lessons with de Sacy, which is why his name does not appear on official documents in Paris, so far as I am aware.

34.   Nicolas Lyon-Caen, "Silvestre de Sacy, savant janséniste?" in *Silvestre de Sacy*, op. cit. note 28, 87–102.

35. For general grammar in the English-speaking world, Hans Aarsleff, *The Study of Language in England, 1780–1860* (London: Athlone Press, 1983), 14–17; Roy Harris and Talbot J. Taylor, *Landmarks in Linguistic Thought: The Western Tradition from Socrates to Saussure* (London: Routledge, 1989), 94–107.

36. *Principles of General Grammar, adapted to the Capacity of Youth, and Proper to Serve as an Introduction to the Study of Languages* (Andover: Flagg, Gould, and Newman, 1834).

37. Jean-Patrick Guillaume, "Silvestre de Sacy lecteur des grammairiens arabes," in *Silvestre de Sacy*, op. cit. note 28, 115–27. De Sacy also edited the "Alfiyyah," a long poem devoted to niceties of Arabic grammar, in use at al-Azhar in his time and well into the 20th century, *Alfiyya ou la quintessence de la grammaire arabe* ... (Paris: Oriental Translation Fund of Great Britain and Ireland, 1833).

38. *Grammaire Arabe* (Paris: Imprimerie royale, 1810), Salisbury owned the 1831 edition.

39. *Calila et Dimna, ou Fables de Bidpai en arabe* ... (Paris: Imprimerie royale, 1816); *Colombe: messagère plus rapide que l'éclair, plus prompte que la nue* ... (Paris: Imprimerie royale, 1805).

40. *Séances de Hariri* ... (Paris: Imprimerie royale, 1822). Only the brilliant iconoclast Arabist Johann Reiske had dared to dismiss Hariri, whose *Maqamat* he had translated into Latin, as simply a "grammatical pedant," *D. Johann Jacob Reiskens von ihm selbst aufgesetzte Lebensbeschreibung* (Leipzig: Gelehrte, 1783), 14, but many of his publications on Arabic literature, extreme rarities even in de Sacy's time, were evidently unknown to the Paris master, and he surely would not have agreed.

41. François Déroche, "La 'chrestomathie arabe' de Silvestre de Sacy," in *Silvestre de Sacy*, op. cit. note 28, 61–72. This offered a wide choice of substantial readings from Arabic literature, with little emphasis on religion, so was precisely what Salisbury had sought to study: Sylvette Larzul, "Silvestre de Sacy et la constitution d'un corpus des belles-lettres arabes," in *Silvestre de Sacy*, op. cit. note 28, 135–51.

42. Hartleben, *Champollion*, op. cit. note 11, 77.

43. Above, note 28.

44. Hartleben, *Champollion*, op. cit. note 11, 79.

45. Ibid., 80.

46. *Bibliothèque de M. le baron Silvestre de Sacy* (Paris: Imprimerie royale, 1842–47). I have used a Yale copy annotated with all prices realized. I suspect it was Salisbury who tried to buy the personal library of Heinrich Fleischer, de Sacy's student and the leading European Arabist of the next generation, until the Prussian government intervened: Heinrich Thorbecke, "Dem Andenken Heinrich Lebenrecht Fleischer's," *Zeitschrift der Deutschen Morgenländischen Gesellschaft* 42 (1888): 695–700 (698).

47. De Sacy's copy of this ultimate collector's item, formerly owned by Tychsen, went to the bibliophile Merlin himself, who catalogued the printed books for the sale, for 201 francs (about $2150 today in terms of buying power of gold). Miroslav Krek, "The Enigma of the First Arabic Book Printed from Movable Type," *Journal of Near Eastern Studies* 38 (1979): 203–12, knew of only eight copies, and none in France. It is surprising that de Sacy's copy did not find its way to the Bibliothèque Nationale.

48. Anthony Grafton, *Forgers and Critics: Creativity and Duplicity in Western Scholarship* (Princeton: Princeton University Press: 1990), 101, with reference to the forged "Berossian" works by Annius of Viterbo. Postel, ever perverse, defended the authenticity of various writings ascribed to Berossos truly or falsely (cited by Grafton, ibid., 149 note 21). Scaliger, for his part, saw Berossos as a reflection of something genuine and very ancient, even if it had no relevant content to modern thought, but his contemporary Casaubon commented, "I don't see of what great use these inventions of foolish peoples are to real history" (ibid., 121). This reads like a dismal epitaph on Assyriology before it had been founded. A close second to Scaliger's comments might be John Selden's tome, *De Dïs Syriis syntagmata II* of 1617, several times reprinted. Americans of Salisbury's time could have known this work through *Fabulous Gods denounced in the Bible, translated from Selden's Syrian Deities by W. A. Hauser* (Philadelphia: Lippincott, 1880). For Selden's book, Jason P. Rosenblatt, *Renaissance England's Chief Rabbi, John Selden* (Oxford: Oxford University Press, 2006), 66, 76–84, who suggests that it was begun about 1613.

49. *The World of Berossos, Proceedings of the 4th International Colloquium on 'The Ancient Near East between Classical and Ancient Oriental Traditions', Hatfield College, Durham, 7th–9th July 2010, Classica et Orientalia 5*, ed. Johannes Haubold, Giovanni Lanfranchi, Robert Rollinger, and John Steele (Wiesbaden: Harrassowitz, 2013). For the Berossian forgeries, Walter Stephens, "From Berossos to Berosus Chaldaeus: The Forgeries of Annius of Viterbo and Their Fortune," ibid., 277–89, who notes that Pseudo-Berossos has probably attracted more commentary than the authentic fragments (ibid., 286). From the Assyriological standpoint, an additional complication is that some ancient authors may have ascribed material to Berossos pseudonymously or alleged that they were quoting a book that they had never in fact read: W. G. Lambert, "Berossus and Babylonian Eschatology," *Iraq* 38 (1976): 171–73.

50. Gustav Dugat, *Histoire des orientalistes de l'Europe du XIIe au XIXe siècle précédée d'une esquisse historique des études orientales* (Paris, Maisonneuve: 1868 [reprint: London: Ganesha, 2003]), vol. 1: 36, quoted by Laurens, op. cit. note 28 (with slight omis-sions), 12.

51. Quoted by Laurens, op. cit. note 28, 20–21.

52. *Memoires sur diverses antiquités de la Perse et sur les médailles de la dynastie des Sassanides, suivis de l'histoire de cette dynastie …* (Paris: Imprimerie nationale exécutive du Louvre, 1793 [reprinted Paris, 2012]). This included a discussion of the inscriptions at Naqsh-i-Rustam. Salisbury's "On the Identification of the Signs of the Persian Cuneiform Alphabet," *Journal of the American Oriental Society* 1/4 (1849): 517–58 (forerunner in *Journal of the American Oriental Society* 1/3 [1848]: 324–28) was the first professional American article on cuneiform; these two show that he had read widely and deeply on the decipherment of Old Persian and Akkadian. His first essay on what would now be considered Assyriology appeared four years later, discussing the recently discovered Black Obelisk of Shalmaneser III: "Colonel Rawlinson's Outlines of Assyrian History Derived from His Latest Readings of Cuneiform," *Journal of the American Oriental Society* 3 (1853): 486–90. For meetings of the American Oriental Society as the sole venue for early Assyriology in the United States, C. Wade Meade, *Road to Babylon: Development of U. S. Assyriology* (Leiden: Brill, 1974), 22–23.

53. Jules Oppert, *Éléments de la grammaire assyrienne* (Paris: Imprimerie impériale, 1860), second edition under the title *Duppe lisan Assur* ... (Paris: Franck, 1868); for Oppert, who likewise began his publishing career with a study of Old Persian, B. André-Salvini, "Oppert, Jules," in *Reallexikon der Assyriologie* (Berlin: De Gruyter, 2003–5), vol. 10: 117–18; Brigitte Lion and Cécile Michel, "Jules Oppert et le syllabaire akkadien," in *Histoires de déchiffrements: Les écritures du Proche-Orient à l'Égée*, ed. Brigitte Lion and Cécile Michel (Paris: Errance, 2009), 81–94. Salisbury regularly purchased the most important Assyriological books of his time. The gift of his magnificent personal library to Yale in 1870 comprised some 4000 monographs, including large folios like Botta's *Nineveh*, as well as 400 volumes of periodicals in complete series, the principal Arabic and Sanskrit works edited by European scholars, together with works "issued from native presses," and ninety Arabic manuscripts, plus a fund of $6000 to enlarge it: Addison Van Name, "The Library," in *Yale College: A Sketch of its History, with Notices of its Several Departments, Instructors, and Benefactors, together with Some Account of Student Life and Amusements,* ed. William L. Kingsley (New York: Henry Holt, 1879), 184–89 (186).

54. Dorothée Metlitsky Finkelstein, *Melville's Orienda* (New Haven: Yale University Press, 1961), 146 note 7.

55. "The pretension implied in my professional title, I think, discouraged me from the first ... I never advanced much beyond the position where I stood at the start, and not being able to keep the sources filled up I never really welcomed any aspirants to take from me what little I knew," Edgerton, op. cit. note 17, 60–61.

56. Salisbury first attempted to resign from the Yale faculty in 1848 ("I have not ... that accuracy and extent of information which are indispensible to the honest profession of familiarity with any branch of learning ..."), Yale University Library RU 164 box 2, but was persuaded to stay on, finally stepping down in 1856. The reader of his summaries of contemporaneous European scholarship and of his essays and translations will hardly agree with him, but will sympathize with his feeling that he could not singlehandedly cover it all.

Assyriological Peripheries
Early Mesopotamian Studies
in Scandanavia

Gojko Barjamovic

We learn that the Mesopotamians mixed chaff into their mud to make their bricks. This chaff seems to have given rise to a discipline called Assyriology, and a literature whose value can be judged by these texts…for what can one say about a language that consists of only breaks and lacunae, and where each word can be read in all kinds of ways, and mean whatever? A language that cannot be translated, unless you know the accepted meaning in advance … And people must have had magnifying glasses built into their eyes, given that they could engrave or press into clay such microscopic signs … Youth, do not study Assyrian, for it is not a language, it is chaff! Just look at this little sign! ➤ It is like a finger pointing to thin ice, the public convenience, or voi ch'entrate. Yet this tiny sign sounds first like this: as, dil, til, dili, ina, ru, rum, salugub, simed, tal. Would you believe this? But it also has other sounds and meanings (ideographic ones). Behold! Aplu = son; Assur = Assur; êdu = single; nadanu = to give. Would you believe in that? … And such rubbish fills a young mind! There can be no doubt, no contradiction, no absurdity, for the Professor has spoken![1]

Such was the frustration of the Swedish playwright August Strindberg, when in 1912 he tried to teach himself cuneiform (using books acquired through mail order), that an essay on his failure covers forty pages. The excerpts quoted here well encapsulate some of the doubt felt by the wider public about the early results of Assyriology. Judging by the date of his diatribe, however, Strindberg was ignorant of the great advances that had been made in the field during the decades prior to his effort. By his time, students of Akkadian had access to glossaries, sign lists, grammars, and other essential tools, and could find support in a series of general works on the history, religion, and art of the region.

Whether or not it was Strindberg's peripheral geographical position in Stockholm that jeopardized his effort is hard to know. Certainly Sweden was a latecomer to ancient Near Eastern studies, compared to the other Nordic countries. In fact, though, scholars based in other parts of Scandinavia had played crucial roles during the formative phase of the discipline.

One key figure was the leader of the geographical explorations of the Royal Danish Arabia Expedition, the Frisian surveyor Carsten Niebuhr.[2] His journeys from 1761 to 1767 brought back copies of ancient inscriptions from Egypt, Yemen, and Persia and included the first reliable facsimiles of inscriptions written in the cuneiform script (see the cover of the present volume). Their publication thus provided the foundation for the decipherment of the Persian cuneiform script by Grotefend during the first decade of the nineteenth century.[3]

The decades between the Napoleonic and Prussian wars were a period of convergence of intellectuals in Copenhagen, numbering, among others, the discoverer of electromagnetism H. C. Ørsted, the poet Hans Christian Andersen, the philosopher Søren Kierkegaard, the sculptor Bertel Thorvaldsen, and the father of the archaeological three-age system, Christian Thomsen. The Danish capital during the last years of absolutism was also home to the comparative linguist and Oriental philologist Ramus Rask, who wrote numerous treatises on ancient chronology and language.

More importantly for the present context, his student Niels Westergaard[4] undertook a three-year expedition to India and Persia (May 1841 to May 1844), supported by the Danish king Christian VIII, to collate the Persepolis cuneiform copies made by Niebuhr. Westergaard also copied for the first time the lengthy inscriptions in Darius I's tomb at Naqs-e Rostam (known as DNa) and brought back a wealth of manuscripts and additional texts he had copied, notably Ashoka's rock inscription at Girnar Hill in India. After his return, Westergaard became a lecturer in Copenhagen, and in 1850 he was promoted to a full professorship in Indian and Oriental philology.

Westergaard gave his copies of the Old Persian texts to his former teacher in Bonn, the celebrated Norwegian scholar Christian Lassen (1800–1876),[5] and devoted himself to the study of the inscriptions in the language we now call Elamite, which was written in the second type of cuneiform script found on the rock monuments in Iran. He was the first to make serious attempts to decipher this more complicated script, consisting of more than 100 characters and lacking the word-dividers of Old Persian. Studying the Naqs-e Rostam text, which contains the names of many lands and peoples, he decisively increased the number of proper names known, and through comparing its Elamite script with the better-known Persian passage, he laid the groundwork for further Elamite studies.

In two long essays, he was able to establish the phonetic value of some 80 characters by comparing proper names with their Old Persian equivalents.[6] On this basis, he tried also to isolate the other single words of the text, to read them, and to establish their meaning. Later, when he examined the more extensive Elamite version of the Behistun text as edited by Edwin Norris in 1855,[7] he could thereby modify considerably the results that his British friend had achieved. Regrettably, his later work remained relatively unknown, owing to its being written in Danish.

The reason Westergaard began publishing in Danish was likely his dismay with both England and Germany after the Prussian War of 1864, which had lost Denmark the duchies of Slesvig-Holsten without the British intervening. On a side note, the British decision to remain neutral in this conflict had been carried forward by Sir Austen Henry Layard, the discoverer of Nineveh, who served as Under-Secretary for Foreign Affairs in the successive administrations of Lord Palmerston and Lord John Russell from 1861 to 1866.[8]

Following the great discoveries of Layard, Botta, Rassam, and Place in the 1840s and 50s, the new discipline of Assyriology came to be taught in Scandinavia almost from the outset. A position was opened in 1883 for Valdemar Schmidt as a docent of Egyptian and Assyrian at the University of Copenhagen.[9] Schmidt acquired substantial collections of Near Eastern artifacts for the National Museum and the Carlsberg Glyptotek, and trained a first generation of Scandinavian cuneiformists, including Niels Rasmussen, who produced in 1897 the first edition of the royal inscriptions of the Assyrian King Shalmaneser III;[10] Gert Howardy, author of the first complete sign list in the field;[11] and the Norwegian scholar A. G. Lie, whose edition of the annals of Sargon II remained the principal one from 1929 until Andreas Fuchs's 1993 publication.[12] However, Schmidt himself was never promoted from his position as docent,[13] and Assyriology remained part of Oriental Philologies, without its own program and exam status until after World War I.

In Finland the situation was different. The pioneer of Assyriology was Karl Frederik Eneberg,[14] who had studied with Oppert in France and published an article on the summary inscription of Tiglath-Pileser III before his life was tragically cut short by his attempt to join George Smith on his famed trip to Nineveh in 1876 to recover the missing part of the Flood tablet. Choosing a northern route through Aleppo, Eneberg reached Mosul while Smith was still in Baghdad, and he seems to have contracted a fatal disease while waiting for the Englishman to arrive.

A more lasting mark on the field was left by Knut Tallqvist,[15] who became the first professor of Assyriology in a Nordic country. He was trained in Berlin and Leipzig by Delitzsch and Schrader, writing a dissertation in 1890 on the language of Late Babylonian contracts. He began teaching in Helsinki a year later and was promoted to full professor in 1899. In addition to his pioneering work on the Babylonian *maqlû*-series, his onomastic research in particular came to have a lasting impact on the field. His work, effectively superseded just two decades ago by the Helsinki-based prosopographical project on the Neo-Assyrian Empire, included two important studies of Neo-Babylonian names (1906) and Neo-Assyrian ones (1914).[16] Tallqvist also wrote a series of general works in Swedish and Finnish, thus starting the important tradition of making the results of Assyriological studies accessible to a wider audience. Unfortunately for Strindberg in Stockholm, this happened only after the playwright had decided to abandon cuneiform studies altogether.

In Norway, the best-known practitioner of Assyriology was Jørgen Alexander Knudtzon, who received his training in London, Paris, Leipzig, and Berlin. He had originally been destined to take over the chair in Semitic Philology in Oslo, but apparently his colleagues found him lacking a "proper theological spirit."[17] Strindberg was perhaps justified in calling Assyriology a discipline of the Philistines. The problem for Knudtzon was that this lack of zeal led the Norwegian government to decide to leave the chair in Semitic Philology vacant, forcing him to depend upon scholarships and private funds until he was finally included in a state grant in 1894 and was named professor of Semitic Languages in 1907.

Knudtzon's early work includes an important two-volume edition in 1893 of Assyrian prayers to the sun-god,[18] as well as a co-authored volume in 1902 on *Die zwei Arzawa-Briefe*.[19] The latter was the first to launch the theory that two of the cuneiform tablets found in 1887 in a pharaonic chancery at the Egyptian site of el-Amarna were written in an Anatolian language that was an early member of the Indo-European family. His proposal was viewed with skepticism at the time, but confirmed by Bedrich Hrozny's 1917 decipherment of Hittite.[20]

Knudzton is first and foremost known for his work on the corpus of Amarna tablets. In 1894, the Norwegian Parliament awarded Knudzton a yearly stipend to travel to all the collections in Egypt and elsewhere that contained Amarna tablets, and to study and publish those texts. The result was the monumental, two-volume edition of *Die el-Amarna Tafeln* (1907–1915), which remains the standard work and the basis of the nomenclature used to this day.[21] It includes 358 of the 382 itemized tablets and fragments now deemed to have come from the site, and since world conditions in the first half of the twentieth century were not conducive to the task of re-collating the tablets, scattered as they are among several museums, his work served as the only systematic philological treatment until Rainey's recent edition.[22]

Knudzton patiently collated all the then-known Amarna texts and fragments, except for the few acquired by C. Murch and M. Chassinat, which ended up in America; in fact he was the last person ever to see some of them. His outstanding ability to read the texts and his thorough mastery of the contents of the archive made his work of inestimable value.[23] Yet, as Knudtzon explained, he was unable, for health as well as financial reasons, to publish hand-copies of the tablets and had to content himself with trans-literations. He died after a period of illness only two years after the publication, while the world around him sank into a shocking theater of violence in World War I.

The war and its aftermath resulted in the disintegration of the international scholarly community that had coalesced around the great centers of learning in imperial Germany. There, all students of Assyriology had come together, including every one of Scandinavia's first-generation Assyriologists, as discussed above.

The new and more nationalistic *Zeitgeist* that followed World War I is perhaps most extremely expressed in the 1925 book by Budge on the *Rise and Progress of Assyriology*.[24] This was basically a hagiography of his British compatriot, Colonel Henry Rawlinson, who is given credit for just about every discovery made in the field of Oriental philology. On the other hand, all that came out of Germany is presented as derivative and poor. In a closing quotation, Budge draws the early Scandinavian Orientalists into his discussion of primacy:

> German and other scholars claim that the works of Rask, Lassen and Wester-gaard were the sources of Rawlinson's success; but Rawlinson had done his work before he saw them or even knew of their existence. And these three scholars were Scandinavians, and not Germans: Assyriology in its early stages owed much to Denmark and very little to Germany. We may note too, that the three greatest Assyriologists in Germany, Strassmaier, Hommel and Bezold, were Bavarians.[25]

In other words, if a German ever did anything right, he was certainly not a Prussian!

The political turmoil in Europe affected Assyriology in Scandinavia in a very direct way. Whereas previously students had flocked to Germany, the years that followed World War I saw the establishment of more localized centers. In Finland, Tallqvist weathered the atrocities of the brutal 1918 civil war that left almost 40,000 people dead in less than four months. Navigating the restructured academic system, he managed to build a successful program and train several new scholars in the field, including Harri Holma and Armas Salonen.[26]

In Norway, on the other hand, Knudtzon's professorship in Semitic philology did not go to a cuneiformist, and in Sweden the study of the ancient Near East continued to be carried out chiefly within the framework of Christian theology. In Denmark, though, the University of Copenhagen managed to convince Valdemar Schmidt to retire in 1922 (at the tender age of 85) so as to allow two new full professorships to open—one in Egyptology in 1924, the other in Assyriology in 1926.

The new Danish professor of Assyriology was Otto Ravn. He was a pupil of Schmidt and Buhl in Copenhagen, but had spent years studying with Jensen in Marburg, Zimmern in Leipzig, Brockelmann in Königsberg, Scheil in Paris, and Pinches and Langdon in London and Oxford. This broad international priming led Ravn to reform the field in Copenhagen, turning it into a modern university discipline with scheduled classes and examination plans.[27] His first graduating student was Thorkild Jacobsen,[28] who received his Mag. Art. degree in 1927 and was immediately sent off to the emerging intellectual powerhouse of the Oriental Institute in Chicago.

Upon his arrival, Jacobsen was required to take an examination to earn an American degree, but Chiera clearly thought that this was a superfluous and somewhat silly exercise. He thus allowed Jacobsen to take exactly the same exam that had been designed for him by Ravn in Copenhagen, and as chance would have it, this template designed by Ravn came to set the precedent for subsequent exams in Chicago and continues to form the basis of the examination that is still in use there.[29]

More significantly for the future of Assyriology, Jacobsen defined for himself a new role as "field Assyriologist" for Chicago's Iraq Expedition of 1929–1937. When Jacobsen left Copenhagen in 1927, Ravn took the opportunity to travel to Iraq and participate in Woolley's excavations of the Royal Tombs at Ur. Jacobsen's approach to the study of the remote past thus seems to owe something to the inspiration of Schmidt and Ravn, although its deeper intellectual foundations of combining textual data and material culture in a synthetic concept of history were developed at Chicago in concert with Frankfort and other colleagues. These ideas came to challenge and redefine the dominant continental tradition of Assyriology as *Editionsphilologie* based solely on textual critique and exegesis. Jacobsen's work at Jerwan and his 1939 Copenhagen *habilitation* on *The Sumerian Kinglist* are examples of his broad approach to history and his intellectual rigor.

Following World War II, Jacobsen became Director of the Oriental Institute and Dean of the Humanities at Chicago. He was also Editor of the Assyrian Dictionary (1955–1959) and held a new position as Professor of Social Institutions (1946–1962). During this period, Jacobsen famously pushed to invite persecuted German Jewish scholars to the Oriental Institute. They came mainly via Turkey, where they had been building up a new university system and training a first generation of scholars after their expulsion from Nazi Germany. Jacobsen was thus able to gather many of the leading scholars of his generation under the same roof, including Benno Landsberger, Hans Gustav Güterbock, and Leo Oppenheim, creating a veritable "golden age" that lasted for a few decades. Jacobsen himself left Chicago in 1962 for a professorship at Harvard University, where he remained until his retirement in 1974.

By that time, Assyriology in Scandinavia was thriving in Copenhagen and Helsinki, and a dedicated position had opened up in Sweden at Uppsala. Jørgen Læssøe followed Ravn in Copenhagen; Åke Sjöberg went to Chicago from Nyberg's Semitics program in Uppsala and then took up a professorship at the University of Pennsylvania; Asger Aaboe came from Copenhagen to Brown and then Yale; and Simo Parpola was appointed extraordinary professor in Helsinki. The 70s, 80s and 90s in many ways represent the corresponding "golden age" of Nordic Assyriology, with four positions in Copenhagen (Jørgen Læssøe, Mogens Trolle Larsen, Aage Westenholz, and Bendt Alster), Olaf Pedersén in Uppsala, Ebbe Knudsen in Oslo, and the very successful Neo-Assyrian Text Corpus Project under the direction of Simo Parpola in Finland.

The situation since the year 2000 looks somewhat bleaker. In Copenhagen the number of professorships has shrunk to one; Helsinki no longer supports a full professor and neither does Uppsala. Semitics in Oslo is run by a linguist. But academic developments are hard to predict and matters may easily change with a substantial grant at any of the four institutions. It would certainly seem premature to go along with Strindberg and to give up on the exasperating "chaff" of Mesopotamia by abandoning

> the Assyrians, so as to turn to the Egyptians, with the brokenness that follows from having been physically intimate with pathological liars. [30]

NOTES

1. *Samlade skrifter av August Strindberg,* vol. 55 (Stockholm: Bonniers, 1912–25), 495–96, 503, 515–16. For the second half of the passage, cf. Mogens Trolle Larsen, *The Conquest of Assyria: Excavations in an Antique Land* (London: Routledge, 1996), 358.

2. Carsten Niebuhr, b. 1733 in the port of Lüdingworth, now part of Cuxhaven at the mouth of the Elbe River; d. 1815 in Meldorf in Ditmarsken, Holsten.

3. Georg Friedrich Grotefend (1775–1853). His first discovery was communicated to the Royal Society of Göttingen in 1802 and reviewed two years later by the Slesvig/Danish Orientalist and Hebrew scholar Oluf Gerhard Tychsen (b. in Tønder 1734, Prof. of Oriental Languages at Bützow and later Rostock). Tychsen had worked on the copies brought back by Niebuhr (and also the less reliable versions made by the Dutch traveller Cornelius de Bruijn, b. 1652), and surmised that their three columns must contain three different forms of cuneiform writing. Cf. O. G. Tychsen *De cuneatis inscriptionibus Persepolitanis lucubratio* (Rostock: Ex officina libraria Stilleriana, 1798). Another German/Danish scholar, Bishop Frederik Münter (1761–1830), correctly concluded that the individual words in the text were divided from one another by a wedge (Tychsen had suggested that they were sentence dividers). Cf. Münter, "Undersögelse om de persepolitanske Inscriptioner," *Det Kongelige Videnskabers-Selskabs Skrivter for Aar 1800,* Vol. 1, 257f., and A. H. Sayce *The Archaeology of the Cuneiform Inscriptions* (London: Society for Promoting Christian Knowledge, 1908), 10ff. See also Jean Bottéro, *Mesopotamia: Writing, Reasoning, and the Gods* (Chicago and London: University of Chicago Press, 1992), 56. Niebuhr himself had observed that all three columns must be read from left to right.

4. Niels Westergaard (1815–1878), Danish Orientalist born in Copenhagen; cf. also Larsen, *Conquest of Assyria,* 85–86.

5. Himself a teacher of the French pioneer of Assyriology, Jules Oppert, who was introduced to the field of cuneiform studies by reading with Lassen Niebuhr's and Westergaard's copies of the Persian royal inscriptions.

6. "Zur Entzifferung der Achämenidischen Keilschrift zweiter Gattung," *Zeitschrift für die Kunde des Morgenlandes* 6 (1845): 337–466 and *Om den Anden eller den sakiske Art af akhæmenidernes Kileskrift* (Copenhagen: Bianco Luno, 1854).

7. Edwin Norris, "Memoir on the Scythic Version of the Behistun Inscription," *Journal of the Royal Asiatic Society* 15 (1855): 1–213.

8. Larsen, *Conquest of Assyria,* 360 and cf. http://hansard.millbanksystems.com/people/mr-austen-layard/1864 for the Official Report of debates in Parliament. Little did Layard foresee that the decision to keep England neutral in the war would lead to a stagnation in Elamite studies that lasted basically until the French excavations of Susa a generation later.

9. Johan Henrik Gamst Valdemar Schmidt (1836–1925); cf. Torben Holm-Rasmussen, *Dansk Biografisk Leksikon* (3. udgave) 1979–1984, vol. 21, 264–65 and Jakob Flygare, "Assyriologiens Historie i Danmark," *Papyrus* 2006.1: 28–33.

10. Niels Rasmussen, *Salmanasser den II's indskrifter i kileskrift, transliteration og translation, samt commentar til monolith-indskriften, col. 1, af N. Rasmussen; udg. med understottelse af Carlsbergfondets midler* (Copenhagen: Kayser, 1897).

11. Gert Howardy, *Clavis cuneorum. sive, Lexicon signorum assyriorum linguis latina, britannica, germanica, sumptibus Instituti Carlsbergici hauniensis compositum a G. Howardy* (London: H. Milford, 1904–1933).

12. Arthur Godtfred Lie, *The Inscriptions of Sargon II, King of Assyria / transliterated and translated with notes by A.G. Lie* (Paris: Geuthner, 1929); Andreas Fuchs, *Die Inschriften Sargons II aus Khorsabad* (Göttingen: Cuvillier Verlag, 1993).

13. Schmidt did hold rank as titulary professor (Professors Navn) since 1869, and was to be properly titled as 'Højædle og velbyrdige' (High and Noble).

14. Cf. E. A. Wallis Budge, *The Rise and Progress of Assyriology* (London: Martin Hopkinson, 1925), 116–17; Sanna Aro, *Kansallisbiografia* (e-version 2011); Aro and Raija Mattila, "Assyriological Studies in Finland," *Proceedings of the Foundation of the Finnish Institute in the Middle East* 1 (2007): 7–9.

15. Aro and Mattila, "Studies in Finland," 9–11.

16. Knut Leonard Tallqvist, *Neubabylonisches Namenbuch* (Acta Societatis scientiarum fennicae 42.2) (Helsinki: Finnish Oriental Society, 1906) and *Assyrian Personal Names* (Acta Societatis scientiarum fennicae 43.1) (Helsinki: Finnish Oriental Society, 1914).

17. Kjell Artun, "Jørgen Knudtzon," *Norsk Biografisk Leksikon* (2009 edition), which also provides a full list of his writings.

18. Jørgen A. Knudzton, *Assyrische Gebete an den Sonnengott für Staat und königliches Haus aus der Zeit Asarhaddons und Asurbanipals; mit Unterstutzung der Universität Kristiania* (Leipzig: Pfeiffer, 1893).

19. Knudzton, *Die zwei Arzawa-briefe, die ältesten urkunden in indogermanischer sprache. Mit bemerkungen von Sophus Bugge und Alf Torp* (Leipzig: Hinrich, 1902).

20. Bedrich Hrozny, *Die Sprache der Hethiter, ihr Bau und ihre Zugehörigkeit zum indogermanischen Sprachstamm: ein Entzifferungsversuch* (Leipzig: Hinrich, 1917).

21. Knudzton, *Die El-Amarna-Tafeln, mit Einleitung und Erläuterungen. Herausgegeben von J.A. Knudtzon. Anmerkungen und Register bearbeitet von Otto Weber und Erich Ebeling*, Vorderasiatische Bibliothek, vol. 2 (Leipzig: Hinrich, 1907–1915).

22. Anson F. Rainey, z"l, *The El-Amarna Correspondence: A New Edition of the Cuneiform Letters from the Site of El-Amarna based on Collations of all Extant Tablets. Collated, Transcribed, and Translated by Anson F. Rainey Z"l*. Vol. 1 edited by William M. Schniedewind; Vol. 2 edited and completed by Zipora Cochavi-Rainey (Leiden: Brill, 2014). On the role of Knudzton, cf. esp. vol. 1, 6–9.

23. Rainey, *Amarna*, 7f.

24. Supra n. 14; cf. Lassen, *Conquest of Assyria*, 355–56.

25. Supra n. 14, 295.

26. Aro and Mattila, "Studies in Finland," 11–16.

27. Jørgen Læssøe and Thorkild Jacobsen, "Otto E. Ravn," *Dansk Biografisk Leksikon, 3. udgave.* (Copenhagen: Gyldendal 1979–84); e-version: http://denstoredanske.dk/

Dansk_Biografisk_Leksikon/Historie/Assyriolog/Otto_E._Ravn.

28.   Læssøe, "Assyriologi i Danmark," in *Assyriologien i Danmark*, ed. Læssøe (Copen-hagen: Købehavns Universitets Assyriologiske Institut, 1977), 22.

29.   Chiera had just been appointed to replace D. D. Luckenbill, who had died suddenly, when he too died. Since Jacobsen was then left with no Assyriologist to work with, he ended up taking his Chicago Ph.D. in Syriac under Martin Sprengling, with a thesis on a commentary on the Book of Job. He returned to Assyriology only through his work with Frankfort in the 1930s. For a brief biography of Jacobsen, with further references and a complete bibliography, see Tzvi Abusch and Bendt Alster's intro-ductory remarks in *Riches Hidden in Secret Places: Ancient Near Eastern Studies in Memory of Thorkild Jacobsen*, ed. Abusch (Winona Lake, Ind.: Eisenbrauns, 2002). See also Jacobsen's autobiographical essay, "Searching for Sumer and Akkad," in *Civilizations of the Ancient Near East*, vol. IV, ed. Jack M. Sasson (New York: Scribner's, 1995), 2743–52.

30.   *Skrifter Strindberg* (supra n. 1), 516.

Between Microphilology, Academic Politics, and the Aryan Jesus
Paul Haupt, Hermann Hilprecht, and the Birth of American Assyriology
Eckart Frahm

As Karl Marx once famously claimed, "Hegel remarks somewhere that all facts and personages of great importance occur, as it were, twice. He forgot to add: the first time as tragedy, the second as farce."[1] Twice in the course of the sixty years that passed from the 1880s to the 1940s, groups of cuneiform scholars who had received their academic formation at the Institute for Semitic Studies at the University of Leipzig in Germany later went to the United States, where they shaped in decisive ways the development of Assyriology in the New World.[2] The first group comprised several students, both Germans and Americans, of Friedrich Delitzsch, the leading Assyriologist of the last quarter of the nineteenth century. They became important representatives of their academic discipline in various universities on the East Coast during the 1880s. In the 1940s, two additional cuneiform scholars with roots in Leipzig came to the States, after a long odyssey that had initially brought them to Ankara in Turkey: the Assyriologist Benno Landsberger, who had taught at Leipzig in the 1920s and 1930s,[3] and his student Hans Gustav Güterbock, one of the leading Hittitologists of the twentieth century.[4] Both of them became eminent scholars at the Oriental Institute in Chicago.

Marx, in the aforementioned quotation, was referring to world-historical events, such as Napoleon's two exiles, and one can obviously question whether the two episodes of Leipzig Orientalists crossing the Atlantic live up to this mark; but for the field of Assyriology in the United States, they certainly did have a transformative effect.[5] Contrary to what Marx claims, it seems, however, that it was rather the second of these exoduses, and not the first, that can be characterized as a tragedy: Landsberger and Güterbock fled Germany in the mid-1930s because the Nazi regime forced them to leave. The earlier exodus, in contrast, while not without serious academic implications, offers certain farce-like elements, especially in the case of its two chief protagonists, Paul Haupt and Hermann Hilprecht.

In this article, I will focus on the careers of these latter two scholars, following them in the spirit of Plutarch's *Parallel Lives*. The connection between Haupt and Hilprecht on the one hand and Edward Salisbury (1814–1901), the main character of this volume, on the other is not an immediate one, which comes as no surprise considering that the field of ancient Near Eastern Studies in the United States in general was not directly linked to Salisbury. Salisbury, after all, was a scholar of Arabic and Sanskrit. He had received his education with European Orientalists such as Silvestre de Sacy and Franz Bopp, who were specialists in Persian, Arabic, and Sanskrit, but not in the languages and scripts of the ancient Near East, deciphered only after or towards the end of their respective careers. Even so, we shall see that certain links between Salisbury and the American careers of our two German Assyriologists do exist.[6]

As noted above, Haupt and Hilprecht were both students of Friedrich Delitzsch, the founder of Assyriology as a rigorous academic discipline. Earlier scholars such as George Smith, the British decipherer of the famous "flood tablet" of the Gilgamesh epic and many other texts, had to a significant extent drawn on their intuition when translating cuneiform tablets. Delitzsch, who was born in 1850 and died in 1922, put the field on a firm philological footing by authoring the first systematic Akkadian grammar (1889), the first dictionary (1894–96), and the first text book (1876–1912). Only later in his life did he become preoccupied with the idea that he had to prove the derivative character of the Hebrew Bible vis-à-vis Mesopotamian civilization.[7]

Like Salisbury, Delitzsch had initially studied not only Semitic languages but also Sanskrit, and had planned to work on a *habilitation* thesis in this latter field. But he changed his mind after the Hebrew Bible scholar and Assyriologist Eberhard Schrader, during a momentous meeting with him in 1873 at the "Gasthof zur Sonne" in Jena (see Figure 1), told him that the future belonged to the emerging field of cuneiform studies. Delitzsch's scholarly turn signaled a paradigmatic shift in German academia: the study of classical India and Persia, which had been so central during the first half of the nineteenth century, especially during the Romantic era, became increasingly sidelined, while interest in the ancient Near East, and funding for the new field, steadily increased.

Delitzsch received his "venia legendi" at the University of Leipzig in 1874 and became Professor Extraordinarius at the same institution in 1877. He was an engaging teacher and soon gathered around himself a circle of gifted students, both from Germany and from other countries, including the United

States. The former included Fritz Hommel, Paul Haupt, Carl Bezold, Peter Jensen, Hermann Hilprecht, Franz Heinrich Weißbach, and Heinrich Zimmern, the latter Alfred Boissier, Knut Tallqvist, and the Americans Edward J. and Robert Francis Harper, David Gordon Lyon, Ira Maurice Price, Hugo Radau, and Samuel Alden Smith, among others.[8] Lyon, who received his Ph.D. in 1882 and afterwards taught at Harvard as Hollis Professor of Divinity, is sometimes called the "Father of American Assyriology."[9] But the impact that two of Delitzsch's German students, namely Haupt and Hilprecht, had on the development of the field in the United States was far greater, even though their history was not one of unmitigated success.

FIGURE 1. Plaque memorializing the 1873 meeting between Eberhard Schrader and Friedrich Delitzsch at the "Gasthof zur Sonne" in Jena. Photo by Jana Matuszak.

American scholars and clergymen of the mid-nineteenth century had considered Germany "a land of cloudy metaphysics and learned atheism," to quote the New England minister and educator Bela Bates Edwards (1802–1852).[10] But over the following decades this attitude changed. German "Wissenschaft," and the way it was organized, became more and more a model for other nations, so much so that in 1867 John Robert Seeley, an English essayist, historian, and professor of modern history at the University of Cambridge, famously claimed, "As a rule, good books are in German."[11] This perception resonated also in the United States, not least in the field of Oriental Studies, where, to a significant extent thanks to Salisbury, a more secular approach was increasingly adopted.[12] The hiring of Haupt and Hilprecht by prominent American universities was a consequence of this new academic paradigm.

★ ★ ★

Paul Haupt (Figure 2) was born in 1858 in the German city of Görlitz and died in 1926 in Baltimore.[13] He studied Semitic languages in Berlin and Leipzig and completed his dissertation, *Die sumerischen Familiengesetze*, in 1878, under the supervision of Delitzsch. Throughout his scholarly career he remained a collaborator and close friend of his teacher.[14] Since 1881, he served as editor, together with Delitzsch, of the *Assyriologische Bibliothek* and since 1889 also of the *Beiträge zur Assyriologie und vergleichenden semitischen Sprach-wissenschaft*. His 1882 edition of Akkadian and Sumerian cuneiform texts from the British Museum (*Akkadische und sumerische Keilschrifttexte*), the first volume of the *Assyriologische Bibliothek*, was a pioneering work, as was his 1880 study of the Sumerian Emesal dialect.

FIGURE 2. Portrait of Paul Haupt, painted by his son and dedicated to Johns Hopkins University by students and colleagues on February 22, 1923. Reproduced from *Oriental Studies Published in Commemoration of the Fortieth Anniversary (1883–1923) of Paul Haupt as Director of the Oriental Seminar of the Johns Hopkins University, Baltimore, Md.*, ed. C. Adler and A. Ember (Baltimore: The Johns Hopkins Press, 1926), frontispiece.

Haupt, who had written his first article in English,[15] served as an unpaid lecturer ("Privatdozent") at the University of Göttingen from 1880 to 1883 and continued to teach there during the summer months until 1889. But in 1883, he accepted a position at the newly founded Johns Hopkins University in Baltimore, where he became a professor of Assyriology and the founding director of the Oriental Seminary. During the six years that he taught both in Göttingen and in Baltimore, Haupt was jokingly called by some of his colleagues "Professor auf beiden Hemisphären" ("professor of both hemispheres").[16]

Haupt owed his prestigious position at Johns Hopkins, which he assumed before he had reached the age of twenty-five, at least indirectly to the renewed interest in Oriental studies that Salisbury, through his work at Yale, had sparked in the United States. The connection is made explicitly in a speech given in 1923 on the occasion of the dedication of a portrait of Haupt by Cyrus Adler, Haupt's first graduate student:

> As the theological seminaries grew into separate institutions or departments, the study of Hebrew in the colleges and universities [in the U.S.] began to decline, but here and there, and most notably at Yale,—which under the inspiration, first of Ezra Stiles, later of Salisbury and Whitney and of the American Oriental Society, formed a most distinguished center for Semitic study—the study of Arabic as well as Hebrew was pursued. From Yale came the first president of Johns Hopkins University, Daniel C. Gilman, and I ascribe it to this fact ... that Johns Hopkins was a pioneer in ... Semitic study ....[17]

Gilman, more prominently showcased in this appreciation than Salisbury, was a multifaceted personality. One of the founders of "Skull and Bones" (Yale's most notorious secret society) while still in New Haven, he had early in his career contemplated a career as a minister and was no stranger to Oriental studies; he served, in fact, as president of the American Oriental Society from 1893 to 1906. He was also a great believer in the German university system and its emphasis on original research rather than the teaching of culture and moral values, which played such a central role in Anglo-American higher education. Given this background, it is not that surprising that Gilman worked hard to bring Haupt to Johns Hopkins.[18]

Haupt had a successful career at his new academic home and published a number of important books and articles during his early years in the New World. His most significant monograph was *Das babylonische Nimrodepos* (published in installments from 1884 to 1891), the first serious attempt to assemble all the manuscripts belonging to what we know today as the Epic of

Gilgamesh. Haupt was also an effective teacher, offering, among other things, the first course in Sumerian ever taught in the United States. Among his students who later had distinguished careers, the most prominent was William F. Albright, who received his Ph.D. from Johns Hopkins in 1916 and became the founding father of a new school of biblical archaeology.[19] Even though Haupt's relationship with his students—who nicknamed him "Lord Yahweh" —was not free of tensions, not least because of Haupt's penchant for theological speculation, his occasional bullying, and his disregard for Puritan sensibilities,[20] the students respected him for his philological acumen.

Haupt also tried to initiate a large excavation project, which he hoped to realize with help from the Smithsonian Institution and government support; the site he had set his eyes on was Ur. When this project failed to materialize, he promoted, in an 1892 German-language publication,[21] a somewhat troubling colonial-archaeological scheme: in order to pave the way for the emigration of persecuted Jews from Russia to the area between Nisibis and Nineveh in northern Mesopotamia or, alternatively, to central Iraq. Haupt suggested sending to the region a reconnaissance team including, among others, three Assyriologists to explore the situation on the ground and at the same time excavate and acquire ancient artifacts.[22]

Not surprisingly—and for good reasons—this plan likewise failed to gain traction. Very much to Haupt's chagrin, it was Hilprecht's name and not his that became inextricably linked to the first major American archaeological project in the Middle East: the excavations at Nippur undertaken under the auspices of the University of Pennsylvania in Philadelphia.[23]

★ ★ ★

Hermann Hilprecht (Figure 3), one year younger than Haupt, was born in Hohenerxleben in Germany in 1859 and died in Philadelphia in 1925.[24] He received his Ph.D. in Leipzig in 1883, became an Old Testament instructor in Erlangen in 1885, and went to Philadelphia in 1886. He initially served as the editor of the *Sunday School Times* but was soon appointed professor of Assyriology at the University of Pennsylvania and, in 1887, curator of the university's Semitic Museum.

The timing of his appointment could not have been more fortunate for Hilprecht. In 1888, the *Babylonian Exploration Fund* of the University of Pennsylvania (which had been established in the previous year with support from the wealthy, religiously minded New York financier Edward White Clark, who wished the United States to compete with the European colonial powers in their quest for antiquities in the Middle East) initiated excavations, first under the direction of John Peters and later of John Henry Haynes, at the site of the ancient city of Nippur in southern Iraq. Peters, a New York Episcopal clergyman, had studied at Yale with Salisbury's student William Dwight Whitney, a Sanskritist, and also held a degree in Hebrew. Hilprecht was asked to become the expedition's co-Assyriologist, even though his delicate health made him quite unsuited for fieldwork.

FIGURE 3. Hermann Vollrath Hilprecht, sporting a fez, in his study in Constantinople in the 1890s. Courtesy University of Pennsylvania Museum of Archaeology and Anthropology, UPM Image #102207.

The expedition was marred by numerous mishaps, including the burning of the first expedition's camp by warring Arab tribes. Nonetheless, the team uncovered in the course of four seasons of work huge numbers of clay tablets inscribed with important literary, religious, and archival texts. Hilprecht, who spent little time at the site and instead stayed in Constantinople, managed to convince the Turkish authorities, most importantly Osman Hamdi Bey—

since 1881 director of the Imperial Ottoman Museum—to allow transfer of many of the tablets to Philadelphia. There, undeterred by considerable difficulties, he initiated the impressive series "Babylonian Expedition of the University of Pennsylvania," which provided descriptions and autographs of numerous Nippur texts. The three volumes authored by Hilprecht himself are characterized by Rykle Borger in his *Reallexikon* entry on Hilprecht as "truly excellent" ("vorzüglich").[25]

★ ★ ★

In their own ways, both Haupt and Hilprecht were masters of microphilology and successful scholars with impressive academic careers. But each man also experienced, later in life, some serious setbacks that were, to some extent, rooted in their inability to reconcile strong feelings of personal and national pride with the roles they had assumed in their American academic institutions.

In his *Reallexikon* entry on Haupt, Borger has little positive to say about the Assyriological work Haupt did during the second half of his life: "die assyriologischen Beiträge aus seiner zweiten Lebenshälfte sind freilich entbehrlich."[26] Haupt focused now on the Old and the New Testaments, working, among other things, on his "Polychrome Bible," an edition of the Hebrew Bible that sought to indicate different manuscript traditions through sophisticated use of a color code. But he also began to promote a number of radical ideas.

During his years in Göttingen in the 1880s, Haupt had come into close contact with Paul de Lagarde (1827–1891),[27] a respected Orientalist and Septuagint scholar, but also one of the founding fathers of nineteenth- and twentieth-century German anti-Semitism.[28] Lagarde sought to establish a German national religion and advocated for the mass deportation of German and European Jews to Palestine or Madagascar. Lagarde's writings shaped central ideas of the prominent anti-Semitic Anglo-German philosopher Houston Steward Chamberlain (1855–1927) and of Alfred Rosenberg (1893–1946), one of the leading ideologues of the National Socialist movement, but also had an impact on the thinking of the cultural Zionist Martin Buber (1878–1965).[29]

In 1880, Lagarde had helped Haupt receive his *venia legendi* at Göttingen (even though only in Assyriology and not in Semitic languages, which severely restricted Haupt's ability to make a living with his teaching), and he wrote several letters of recommendation for him, including one in which he called him "the only Assyriologist not only in Germany but in Europe who has a future."[30] Even after Haupt had assumed his position in Baltimore in

1883, his relationship with Lagarde remained close. In 1891, the year Lagarde died, Haupt dedicated to him his *magnum opus, Das babylonische Nimrodepos*, and arranged the sale of Lagarde's private library for 30,000 marks to New York University, where together with Lagarde's desk chair it was maintained until the 1950s as a separate unit.[31]

Haupt's admiration for Lagarde and his ideas is apparent from his promotion of the Jewish colonization scheme described above,[32] but also from the scholarly work he pursued during his later years. His "Polychrome Bible" project was clearly inspired by Lagarde's attempt to produce a critical edition of the Septuagint—and turned out to be an equally over-ambitious endeavor. Haupt went further, however. He also began to work on issues closely related to some of Lagarde's radical Germanic and anti-Jewish beliefs. Starting in 1908, Haupt published several articles, some in popular and others in scholarly journals, in which he claimed that Jesus was not of Semitic descent but rather Aryan.[33] This idea was not entirely new; it had previously been advocated by Chamberlain.[34] But Haupt now supported it with the ostensibly scholarly argument that Assyrian kings had once deported large numbers of Iranians to Galilee, the putative birthplace of Jesus. Haupt's ideas resonated strongly in the politically charged debate about the "Aryan Jesus," a debate eagerly followed not only in Germany.[35] During the "Third International Congress on the History of Religions," which took place in 1908 at Oxford, some prominent participants considered Haupt's lecture on "The Ethnology of Galilee" "sensational" and continued to talk about it "in the hotel and in the street," after further discussion of Haupt's central ideas in the conference room had been "suppressed."[36] Haupt's hypotheses were taken up also by his former teacher, Delitzsch, who in his later publications, especially in *Die große Täuschung* ("The Great Lie") from 1921, argued that the Old Testament had been composed by a deeply deceitful nation and should be banned from Christian teachings. In the United States, in contrast, Haupt's ideas were mostly met with strong reservation.

It is remarkable, and in need of more exploration,[37] to what extent German scholars of Semitic languages such as Delitzsch, Lagarde, and also Haupt—who as a schoolboy had learnt Hebrew from the local rabbi who was also the father of his favorite playmate[38]—were at the forefront of promoting a theological and to some extent racial anti-Judaism that within a few years' time would become one of the sources of Nazi dogma. It should not be overlooked, however, that Haupt occasionally also expressed admiration for

Jewish culture and held, altogether, a somewhat ambivalent attitude towards it.[39]

★ ★ ★

Hermann Hilprecht remained unimpressed by the ideological agendas pursued by Haupt and Delitzsch. In contrast to Delitzsch, Hilprecht, who had trained as a Lutheran minister, believed that Mesopotamian civilization, while ancient, was also morally corrupt and fundamentally inferior to the world of the Bible. Hilprecht had been critical of Delitzsch from fairly early on, despite the fact that Delitzsch had written him a letter of recommendation when he applied for the position in Philadelphia. Tensions between the two increased when Hilprecht, in 1901, complained about alleged attempts by Delitzsch to have his German students copy cuneiform texts from French and American excavations.[40]

In 1903, Hilprecht was summoned by the German Kaiser's senior court chaplain ("Oberhofprediger") Ernst (von) Dryander to defend the Bible against the ideas expressed by Delitzsch in his notorious "Babel und Bibel" lecture the previous year.[41] Hilprecht did so in a lecture of his own that he gave in the Domstift in Berlin on February 1, 1903, in the presence of the German empress Auguste Victoria, the Kaiser's wife, and other high-ranking dignitaries and academics, but not Wilhelm II himself.[42] Delitzsch did not attend the lecture either, hardly a surprising decision given that he thought his relationship with Hilprecht had by now reached a point where he felt inclined to challenge his opponent to a duel with pistols.[43] Later that year, Hilprecht took steps that led to the cancellation of a trip that Delitzsch had planned to the United States;[44] Delitzsch would not visit the New World before the winter of 1905/1906, when he gave a lecture at Columbia University.[45]

Hilprecht could boast of considerable philological achievements, and his restraint in the controversy about "Babel und Bibel" was prudent. But these credentials did not save him from eventually getting into major trouble in Philadelphia. The reasons for his fall lay in his narcissistic self-centeredness and his aggressive attitude towards his colleagues. In the eleven years of the Nippur excavations, Hilprecht had visited Nippur only twice, and on both occasions had apparently made "brutta figura." At some point during his first stay in the field, for example, he fell from his horse, which was appropriately named "Marduk," into a shallow river and started screaming for his life even though there was no danger at all. Yet despite his own personal shortcomings, Hilprecht constantly questioned the competence of the Nippur excavators, notably Peters and Haynes, and claimed for himself all the spectacular finds the excavations had yielded. Understandably, his comportment did not help him secure the affections of his archaeologist colleagues, especially Peters, who reported the unfortunate episode with the horse in his 1897 book about Nippur.[46] For a while, public opinion and the local press sided with Hilprecht. But when Hilprecht falsely claimed in his 1903 book *Explorations in Bible Lands* that the 23,000 tablets found at Nippur during the last excavation season (1898 to 1900) originated in a temple library, his opponents launched a major campaign against him.[47]

In 1905, Hilprecht was cleared of the charges raised against him in a formal inquiry that investigated his scholarly work and the way he had dealt with the Nippur tablets; but this proved only temporary relief. Almost all major Orientalists in the United States remained opposed to him, as is indicated by the fact that the 1909 "Festschrift" organized for Hilprecht's fiftieth birthday[48] was published in Germany and did not include a single contribution by an American in Hilprecht's field.[49] One year later, in the spring of 1910, Hilprecht went abruptly on a trip to Europe, with the keys to the tablet storeroom in his pocket. The director of the University Museum forcefully opened the door to the room and found the tablets poorly conserved. Hearing of this intrusion, Hilprecht resigned from his professorship in protest, thus effectively ending his academic career. When German and other European Assyriologists unsuccessfully questioned Hilprecht's dismissal in a 1911 letter, Delitzsch's signature was notably absent, a not surprising omission considering how strained had become his relationship with his former pupil.[50]

★ ★ ★

Hilprecht had not only trouble with his colleagues but also with his students, even though he seems to have taught them well the fundamentals of Assyriological research. One of his students was Albert Tobias Clay (1866–1925), who in 1898 published together with Hilprecht an edition of Late Babylonian business documents from Nippur as volume 8 of the *Babylonian Expedition* series.[51] In 1899, Clay became lecturer in Assyriology at Penn, where he taught for the next eleven years, and in his 1907 book, *Light on the Old Testament from Babel*, he supported the arguments his teacher had raised against Delitzsch. Yet he was not happy about having to work under Hilprecht, who constantly interfered in his work. Colleagues remarked that Hilprecht "has taken the heart out of Clay, who is greatly depressed."[52]

Clay was, therefore, understandably delighted when he received an opportunity to leave Philadelphia for Yale, the university where serious Oriental studies in the United States had been initiated more than half a century earlier, under Salisbury and Whitney. Clay knew the New York-based industrialist and financier J. Pierpont Morgan and had helped him assemble a collection of cuneiform tablets. In 1909, Morgan provided the means to create at Yale a Babylonian Collection and an endowed chair in Assyriology, to which Clay was appointed the following year.

Despite his dislike for Hilprecht, Clay brought to Yale certain traditions he had absorbed from his teacher, traditions Hilprecht himself had adopted, at least in part, during the 1880s as a member of Delitzsch's "Leipzig School." Besides high philological standards, these traditions included the typical "Assyriological seminar" setting, with library, tablets, and classroom located in close proximity (a situation fortunately still in place at Yale today), and the habit of playfully inscribing clay tablets, on the occasion of birthdays and other anniversaries, with compliments and good wishes in cuneiform (see Figure 4).[53]

On the whole, however, it seems fair to say that with Clay arriving at Yale, and Haupt and Hilprecht entering their twilight years, a new phase of American Assyriology had begun. On April 2, 1918, towards the end of the first World War—which massively exacerbated anti-German sentiments in the United States[54]—Charles Torrey, Yale's professor of Semitic languages and a friend of Clay's, advocated in the presidential address he delivered in New Haven to the American Oriental Society that American Oriental studies should finally become independent of German models, not least because of the rising anti-Semitism that permeated the works of German Assyriologists and Hebrew Bible scholars.[55] No longer was the United States to remain a German "intellectual colony," "eine geistige Kolonie," as the historian Richard M. Meyer had called it a few years before.[56]

German Assyriology, as I have pointed out above, gained weight again in the United States in later years. But during the early 1920s, a distinctive era of the field had clearly come to an end. It had been a formative era in many respects, even a coming of age. But it had also been a period marred by scholarly arrogance, personal vendettas, and ideological delusions to a significant extent generated by the *furor teutonicus* that its two protagonists, Haupt and Hilprecht, so amply displayed.[57]

FIGURE 4. Clay tablet written by Albert Clay to Charles Torrey in 1911.
Photo by E. Frahm. Copyright: Yale Babylonian Collection.

NOTES

1. The quotation is from the beginning of Chapter 1 of Marx's essay *Der 18. Brumaire des Louis Bonaparte*, published in 1852.

2. Overviews of the history of Assyriology at Leipzig include M. Müller, "Die Keilschriftwissenschaften an der Leipziger Universität bis zur Vertreibung Landsbergers im Jahre 1935," *Wissenschaftliche Zeitschrift der Karl-Marx-Universität Leipzig* 28 (1979): 67–86, and M. P. Streck, "Altorientalistik," in *Geschichte der Universität Leipzig 1409–2009, Vol. 4: Fakultäten, Institute, Zentrale Einrichtungen*, ed. U. von Hehl, U. John, and M. Rudersdorf (Leipzig: Leipziger Universitätsverlag, 2009), 345–66.

3. See J. Oelsner, "Der Altorientalist Benno Landsberger. Wissenschaftstransfer Leipzig – Chicago via Ankara," in *Bausteine einer jüdischen Geschichte der Universität Leipzig*, ed. S. Wendehorst (Leipzig: Leipziger Universitätsverlag, 2006), 269–85.

4. See E. Reiner's obituary of Güterbock in *Proceedings of the American Philosophical Society* 146 (2002): 292–96.

5. For an account of the main stages in the development of the field in the New World from its origins to World War II, see B. R. Foster, "The Beginnings of Assyriology in the United States," in *Orientalism, Assyriology and the Bible*, ed. S.W. Holloway (Sheffield: Sheffield Phoenix Press, 2006), 44–73.

6. I must confess, at this juncture, to a certain degree of "fraud anxiety." Publishing this essay in a volume that includes articles by the leading specialist in German Orientalism in the nineteenth century and one of the most knowledgeable experts on the beginnings of Oriental studies in the United States makes me acutely aware of the fact that I am rather ill equipped to embark on an attempt to bridge these two vast fields. Readers should know that my remarks are based exclusively on published work and not on the study of any archival materials.

7. Delitzsch's career, scholarly contributions, and ideological agendas have been the topic of numerous articles and two monographic studies: R. G. Lehmann, *Friedrich Delitzsch und der Babel-Bibel-Streit* (Freiburg/Schweiz: Universitätsverlag and Göttingen: Vandenhoek & Ruprecht, 1994) and K. Johanning, *Der Bibel-Babel-Streit: Eine forschungsgeschichtliche Studie* (Frankfurt a.M.: P. Lang, 1988). See also B. T. Arnold and D. B. Weisberg, "A Centennial Review of Friedrich Delitzsch's 'Babel and Bibel' Lecture," *Journal of Biblical Literature* 121 (2002): 441–57.

8. See Müller, "Die Keilschriftwissenschaften an der Universität Leipzig," 70; for Alden and Radau, see in more detail B. R. Foster, "Three Forgotten American Assyriologists and their Destinies," in *Digging in the Archives: From the History of Oriental Studies to the History of Ideas*, ed. S. Alaura (Rome: Quasar edizioni, forthcoming).

9. See C. W. Meade, *Road to Babylon: Development of U.S. Assyriology* (Leiden: Brill, 1974), 30–32.

10. Quoted after B. R. Foster, "A Mithridatic Nation: Germany and the Beginnings of American Semitic Scholarship," in *Assyriologica et Semitica: Festschrift für Joachim Oelsner anläßlich seines 65. Geburtstages am 18. Februar 1997*, ed. J. Marzahn and H. Neumann (Münster: Ugarit-Verlag, 2000), 53–64, here 60.

11. See Seeley's "Liberal Education in Universities" (first published in F. W. Farrar's 1867 *Essays on a Liberal Education*); reprinted in: J. R. Seeley, *Lectures and Essays* (London: MacMillan and Co., 1870), 183–216 (the quotation is on 214).

12. Foster, "A Mithridatic Nation," 53.

13. For information on Haupt's career and scholarship, see W. F. Albright, "Professor Haupt as Scholar and Teacher," in *Oriental Studies Published in Commemoration of the Fortieth Anniversary (1883–1923) of Paul Haupt as Director of the Oriental Seminar of the Johns Hopkins University, Baltimore, MD*, ed. C. Adler and A. Ember (Baltimore: The Johns Hopkins Press, 1926), xxi–xxxii; H. Zimmern, "Paul Haupt," *Zeitschrift für Assyriologie* 37 (1927): 295–96; R. Borger, "Ein Jahrhundert Assyriologie an der Universität Göttingen," *Universität Göttingen Informationen* 6 (December 1980): 3–9; and B. R. Foster, "Haupt, P.," in *American National Biography* 10 (New York/Oxford: Oxford University Press, 1999), 320–21. The Haupt Anniversary Volume includes a comprehensive bibliography of the honoree.

14. See Müller, "Die Keilschriftwissenschaften an der Universität Leipzig," 70.

15. Haupt's essay "The Oldest Semitic Verb Form" was published in 1878 in the *Journal of the Royal Asiatic Society*; see Albright, "Professor Haupt as Scholar and Teacher," xxii.

16. See Zimmern, "Paul Haupt," 295.

17. "Cyrus Adler's Address," in *Oriental Studies Published in Commemoration of Paul Haupt*, xvii–xx, here xvii.

18. See J. S. Cooper, "From Mosul to Manila: Early Approaches to Funding Near Eastern Studies Research in the United States," in *The Construction of the Ancient Near East*, Culture and History 11, ed. A. C. Gunter (Copenhagen: Academic Press, 1992), 133–64, here 133–37.

19. See B. O. Long, *Planting and Reaping Albright: Politics, Ideology, and Interpreting the Bible* (University Park, Pennsylvania: The State University Press, 1997) and P. D. Feinman, *William Foxwell Albright and the Origins of Biblical Archaeology* (Berrien Springs, Mich.: Andrews University Press, 2004).

20. Albright often found his teacher's theories poorly founded and occasionally tasteless. Regarding Haupt's claim that Song of Songs 7:2 referred to the vulva and even "the hairs of the vagina," Albright remarked privately: "I doubt very much whether the gifted author would have considered those special features of the Pudenda as such a poetical subject! Prof. H. makes me disgusted sometimes." Albright also complained that Haupt "had flayed him alive" after he had delivered a paper his teacher did not like. See Long, *Planting and Reaping Albright*, 128–29, for references. For obvious reasons, the aforementioned episodes do not feature in Albright's "official" appreciation of Haupt in his essay "Professor Haupt as Scholar and Teacher."

21. P. Haupt, *Über die Ansiedlung der russischen Juden im Euphrat- und Tigris-Gebiete: ein Vorschlag* (Baltimore: Friedenwald Co., 1892).

22. For a detailed assessment of Haupt's never-realized archaeological projects in the Middle East, see Cooper, "From Mosul to Manila," 138–55. In order to finance the scheme, Haupt suggested, besides the sale of agricultural goods, asphalt, and—a

particularly prescient suggestion—petroleum, to trade also in "duplicates" of artifacts found in the course of archaeological excavations: "[G]anz erhebliche Summen könnten durch den Verkauf von *Alterthümern* gewonnen werden. Die werthvollsten Denkmäler aller Art sind im Euphrat- und Tigrisland in solcher Menge vorhanden, dass bei der Vornahme systematischer Ausgrabungen, oder auch nur bei fortschreitender Recultivierung des Bodens, jährlich Tausende von Duplicaten an die verschiedenen amerikanischen und europäischen Museen verkauft werden könnten, ohne ein etwa an Ort und Stelle zu gründendes Althertums-Museum irgendwie zu beeinträchtigen. Fragmente von Thontafeltexten, von denen sich die dazu gehörigen grösseren Stücke bereits Im Britischen Museum befinden, müssten schon im Interesse der Wissenschaft an England verkauft werden" (Haupt, *Über die Ansiedlung*, 12–13).

23. As shown by Cooper ("From Mosul to Manila"), Haupt tried on several occasions to sabotage the University of Pennsylvania's expedition to Nippur.

24. For detailed information on Hilprecht, his career, and his role in the Nippur excavations, see B. Kuklick, *Puritans in Babylon: The Ancient Near East and American Intellectual Life, 1880–1930* (Princeton: Princeton University Press, 1996), 6–7, 33–34, 123–25, and passim. See also B. R. Foster, "Hilprecht, H. V.," in *American National Biography* 10 (New York/Oxford: Oxford University Press, 1999), 825–27; S. Frith, "The Rise and Fall of Hermann Hilprecht," *The Pennsylvania Gazette January–February 2003* (http://www.upenn.edu/gazette/0103/frithsidebar.html); and R. G. Ousterhout, "Archaeologists and Travelers in Ottoman Lands," *Expedition Magazine* 52.2 (July 2010): n. pag. Penn Museum, July 2010 Web. 12 Jan 2017 <http://www.penn.museum/sites/expedition/?p=12804>.

25. R. Borger, "Hilprecht, Hermann Vollrat/Volrath," in *Reallexikon der Assyriologie und Vorderasiatischen Archäologie*, Vol. 4, ed. D. O. Edzard (Berlin/New York: De Gruyter, 1972–1975), 410.

26. R. Borger, "Haupt, Paul," in *Reallexikon der Assyriologie und Vorderasiatischen Archäologie*, Vol. 4, ed. D. O. Edzard (Berlin/New York: De Gruyter, 1972–1975), 175.

27. For the relationship between Lagarde and Haupt, see U. Sieg, *Deutschlands Prophet: Paul de Lagarde und die Ursprünge des modernen Antisemitismus* (München/Vienna: Hanser, 2007), 118, 135, 146–49, 303 (English translation: *Germany's Prophet: Paul de Lagarde and the Origins of Modern Antisemitism* [Waltham, Mass.: Brandeis University Press, 2015]); Albright, "Professor Haupt as Scholar and Teacher," xxiii; and H. Zimmern, "Paul Haupt," *Zeitschrift für Assyriologie* 37 (1927): 296. Zimmern points out that even Haupt's style was strongly influenced by Lagarde.

28. For Lagarde's scholarship and ideological positions, see S. Marchand, *German Orientalism in the Age of Empire* (Cambridge: Cambridge University Press, 2009), 168–74, and Sieg, *Deutschlands Prophet*, passim.

29. See U. Bermbach, *Houston Stewart Chamberlain: Wagners Schwiegersohn – Hitlers Vordenker* (Stuttgart/Weimar: Metzler, 2015), 67, 166, 414, 540, and Sieg, *Deutschlands Prophet*, 292–353.

30. "der einzige Assyriologe nicht blos Deutschlands, sondern Europas, der Zukunft hat" (quoted after Sieg, *Deutschlands Prophet*, 148).

31. See Sieg, *Deutschlands Prophet*, 302–3, and F. Stern, *The Politics of Cultural Despair: A Study in the Rise of the Germanic Ideology* (Berkeley: University of California Press, 1961), 24.

32. Lagarde's influence on Haupt is one of the few things not noted in Cooper's otherwise thoroughly researched "From Mosul to Manila" article. For thoughts on nineteenth-century German Orientalism and its attitudes towards imperialism, see Marchand, *German Orientalism in the Age of Empire*, 333–86.

33. P. Haupt, "Die arische Abkunft Jesu und Seiner Jünger," *Orientalistische Literaturzeitung* 11 (1908): 237–40; id., "Davids und Christi Geburtsort," *Orientalistische Literaturzeitung* 12 (1909): 65–69; id., "The Aryan Ancestry of Jesus," *The Open Court* 23 (1909): 193–209. *The Open Court* was a Chicago journal "devoted to the work of conciliating religion with science"; for a PDF of Haupt's article, see http://www.iapsop.com/archive/materials/open_court/open_court_v23_1909.pdf. The last sentence of the article reads, "It is extremely improbable that Jesus was a son of David; it is at least as probable that he was a scion of [the Median chieftain] Deioces or even a descendant of Spitam, the ancestor of Zoroaster."

34. See Bermbach, *Houston Stewart Chamberlain*, 453–98.

35. See S. Heschel, *The Aryan Jesus: Christian Theologians and the Bible in Nazi Germany* (Princeton: Princeton University Press, 2008), on Haupt's role, see 57. The idea of an Aryan Jesus was later endorsed by many supporters of the pro-Nazi "Deutsche Christen" movement.

36. See M. Richter and B. Hamacher, "Deutsch-englische Mythos-Mythen: Oxford 1908 – universelle und nationale Forschungstraditionen," in *In the Embrace of the Swan: Anglo-German Mythologies in Literature, the Visual Arts and Cultural Theory*, ed. R. Görner and A. Nicholls (Berlin/New York: De Gruyter, 2010), 341–52, here 343–44.

37. But see, for example, Marchand, *German Orientalism in the Age of Empire*, 292–332.

38. See Albright, "Professor Haupt as Scholar and Teacher," xxi.

39. In *The Open Court* 23 (1909): 193, Haupt writes, "Pilate was no doubt responsible for the execution of the Messiah, not the Jews." And in his article "Die Vorfahren der Juden" (*Orientalistische Literaturzeitung* 12 [1909]: 162–63), Haupt links the achievements of the Jews to those of the people of the United States: "Die Lebenskraft und die sonstigen hervorragenden Eigenschaften der jüdischen Rasse beruhen …, ebenso wie die großartige Entwicklung der Vereinigten Staaten von Nordamerika, in erster Linie auf Rassenmischung." Here, even though using racial categories, Haupt is obviously far away from later Nazi ideology. But Haupt also made thoroughly anti-Jewish statements during his life. In a letter to Lagarde from December 28, 1886, he wrote that the Persian king Cyrus would not have managed to conquer Babylon had he not profited from the treachery of what he calls contemptuously "die jüdischen Pfaffen" ("the Jewish clerics"); see Sieg, *Deutschlands Prophet*, 149.

40. See Lehmann, *Friedrich Delitzsch*, 205.

41. Delitzsch delivered this lecture on January 13, 1902 and gave a second lecture on the topic on January 12, 1903.

42. See Lehmann, *Friedrich Delitzsch*, 201–5.

43. Thus in a letter to Felix von Luschan from January 15, 1903; see Lehmann, *Friedrich Delitzsch*, 205.

44. See Kuklick, *Puritans in Babylon*, 126, 221–22. The invitation had come from Morris Jastrow Jr., a colleague of Hilprecht at the University of Pennsylvania and, interestingly, a Jew whose positive attitude towards Delitzsch put him in opposition to both confessional Jews and confessional Protestants.

45. The lecture was sponsored by the *Germanistische Gesellschaft* and took place as part of a program in German cultural history. Other lecturers in the years following included Ludwig Fulda, Carl Hauptmann, Ernst von Wolzogen, and Rudolf Herzog. See A. B. Faust, *Das Deutschtum in den Vereinigten Staaten in seiner Bedeutung für die amerikanische Kultur* (Wiesbaden: Springer, 1912), Vol. 2, 219–20.

46. J. P. Peters, *Nippur – or Explorations and Adventures on the Euphrates: The Narrative of the University of Pennsylvania Expedition to Babylonia in the Years 1888–1890*, Vol. 1 (New York / London: G.P. Putnam's Sons, 1897), 122–23.

47. The so-called "Peters-Hilprecht controversy" has been described in detail by several scholars, most notably by Kuklick, *Puritans in Babylon*, especially pp. 123–40; see also the other references listed in note 24.

48. *Hilprecht Anniversary Volume: Studies in Assyriology and Archaeology Dedicated to Hermann V. Hilprecht upon the Twenty-fifth Anniversary of His Doctorate and His Fiftieth Birthday (July 28) by His Colleagues, Friends and Admirers* (Leipzig: Hinrichs, 1909).

49. As observed by Kuklick, *Puritans in Babylon*, 138.

50. See Foster, "Three Forgotten American Assyriologists," n. 41.

51. On Clay, see B. R. Foster, "Clay, Albert Tobias," in *American National Biography* 5 (New York/Oxford: Oxford University Press, 1999), 17–18, and id., "Albert T. Clay and His Babylonian Collection," in *Beyond Hatti: A Tribute to Gary Beckman*, ed. B. J. Collins and P. Michalowski (Atlanta: Lockwood Press, 2013), 121–35.

52. See Kuklick, *Puritans in Babylon*, 124.

53. The production of such texts at Leipzig is documented by Müller ("Die Keilschriftwissenschaften an der Leipziger Universität," 71, n. 12), who mentions that on the occasion of the 100th anniversary of the C. F. Hinrichs publishing house on August 1, 1891, Rudolph Zehnpfund inscribed a cuneiform tablet with an appreciation composed by Friedrich Delitzsch and Paul Haupt. The tablet is apparently still housed in Leipzig University's "Altorientalisches Institut" (see M. P. Streck, ed., *Die Keilschrifttexte des Altorientalischen Instituts der Universität Leipzig* [Wiesbaden: Harrassowitz, 2011], 3, n. 10). Zehnpfund seems to have been known for his good cuneiform hand: another tablet written by him, an excerpt of various Akkadian epical texts, was given by Haupt, according to a note in the registration book, in December 1890 to the University Museum in Philadelphia, where it bears the museum number CBS 1942 (for information on this and other Philadelphia tablets, I am much indebted to Grant Frame and Ilona Zsolnay). After his arrival in Baltimore, Haupt regularly instructed his students in prose composition in Akkadian and Sumerian (see Albright, "Professor Haupt as Scholar and Teacher," xxxi), and he

continued to write tablets himself. Photographs and translations of a tablet addressed by Haupt in 1899 to Johns Hopkins's president Daniel Gilman, and of a second one he wrote in 1901 for the Classics professor Basil Gildersleeve, are found together with references to earlier treatments of the tablets at http://archaeologicalmuseum .jhu.edu/the-collection/object-stories/recent-re-discoveries/ (accessed 01/21/2017). According to B. R. Foster (pers. comm.), a fragment of the Gilgamesh Epic written by Haupt was later given by him to the Smithsonian.

Hilprecht requested his Philadelphia students to produce clay tablets as well. CBS 1985, for example (photo: http://cdli.ucla.edu/dl/photo/P259176.jpg), is a copy of a Neo-Babylonian economic tablet written, according to its "colophon," by "Clay, the son of Hilprecht" (*[lú]*UMBISAG *ṭi-iṭ-ṭu* A-*šú* *šá* *[I]Hi-il-pe-re-e-eḫ-tú*) in Philadelphia on April(?) 27, AD 1893 (*[uru]pí-il-a-de-el-pí-ia* *[iti]*GU$_4$ UD 27-KÁM MU *lim* 8 *me* 93 *[d]*EN-*nu*), when Clay was 26 years old. It is noteworthy that in this document, Clay defines his relationship to his teacher in filial terms reminiscent of the German "Doktorvater" concept; the two may still have been on fairly cordial terms at this point. After coming to Yale, Clay produced several additional tablets, now housed in the Yale Babylonian Collection. A handcopy of one of them, a letter written by Clay for his friend and colleague Charles Torrey and his wife Marian on June 16, 1911 ("during the third eponymate of [President William Howard] Taft [*[I]ta-ap-ti*]") was published by E. Frahm and M. Jursa, *Neo-Babylonian Letters and Contracts from the Eanna Archive*, Yale Oriental Series – Babylonian Texts, Vol. 21 (New Haven/London: Yale University Press, 2011), no. 43. Assyriologists were not the only late nineteenth- and early twentieth-century scholars who composed texts in the ancient languages they studied; scholars in Classics as well as academics in various other Orientalist disciplines did so as well. A Neo-Coptic letter written in 1882 by the young Egyptologist Adolf Erman to Paul de Lagarde in Göttingen was published by H. Behlmer, "Ein neo-koptischer Brief Adolf Ermans and Paul de Lagarde: Zeugnis für eine wissen-schaftsgeschichtliche Wende in der Erforschung des Koptischen," *Lingua Aegyptia* 11 (2003): 1–12. Similar to what Clay did in the tablet he wrote in Philadelphia, Erman addresses Lagarde as his (beloved) "father" (*apa*) and calls himself the "son" of the older and more prominent scholar, even though he qualifies this as a descent "in spirit" (*m-pneumatikos*). The writing of letters and other texts in ancient languages is one of the few areas where it seems that the highly serious Orientalists of the period before the first World War actually seem to have had some fun. A systematic exploration of the phenomenon would be an interesting project.

55. Note that Hilprecht, who was considered suspiciously pro-German, decided to leave the United States when the war broke out. His wealthy American wife had to reapply for American citizenship when eventually returning to the States in 1920. See Foster, "Three Forgotten American Assyriologists."

56. See C. C. Torrey, "The Outlook for Oriental Studies," *Journal of the American Oriental Society* 38 (1918): 107–20. Torrey's criticism of German scholarship is oblique but impossible to miss. For some comments, see Foster, "The Beginnings of Assyriology in the United States," 50–51.

57. See Richter and Hamacher, "Deutsch-englische Mythos-Mythen," 342.
58. I would like to thank Benjamin R. Foster and Kathryn Slanski for reading a draft of this essay and making a number of valuable suggestions.

APPENDIX I
Salisbury's Letter of Appointment

At a Meeting of the President and Fellows of Yale College in New Haven on this 7th day of August 1841,

Whereas the Arabic and Sanskrit Languages are original and leading Languages of the Eastern Nations, and the study of them is acquiring increasing importance on account of our Missionary efforts and commercial intercourse with those regions, and also has important bearings on our own Language and Literature, as well as on the history of the World,

Voted a Professorship of the Arabic and Sanskrit Languages be established in the theological department of this College,

Whereupon this board proceeded to appoint Edward D. Salisbury, A.M., an alumnus of the College, for said Professorship to give such instruction, from time to time, as may suit his convenience, without the expectation of pecuniary compensation.

This text is taken from the fair copy presented to Salisbury. Note that the scribe got Salisbury's middle initial wrong, which likely dismayed the careful philologist and scholar. Yale University Manuscripts and Archives, MS 429, Box 6, Folder 260.

Salisbury's Seals, 160 Years Later
Two Neo-Assyrian Cylinders
from AOS to YBC

Agnete Wisti Lassen

In 1856, Edward Elbridge Salisbury published "Remarks on Two Assyrian Cylinders Received from Mosûl," the first article devoted to this type of artifact to appear in the United States.[1] His short study was in an early issue of the *Journal of the American Oriental Society*, a learned society founded and sustained in large part through Salisbury's efforts and which he served for many years as president, corresponding secretary, and journal editor. The two cylinder seals were a gift from the recently deceased missionary Reverend Henry Lobdell, M.D., who presented the cylinders, along with various Arabic and Hebrew manuscripts, antique silver coins, and two Assyrian gems to the "Cabinet of the Oriental Society."[2] Lobdell acquired these items during his extended stay at Mosul, where he, along with American colleagues and French rivals, collected antiquities to send back home.[3]

Assyriology was still in its infancy when Salisbury studied these two seals. The Akkadian language was only officially deciphered in 1857, the year after his publication, when the Royal Asiatic Society in London presented a newly discovered cuneiform text to four independent experts and a jury declared the translations to be in so close agreement that the script could be considered deciphered. Just a few years earlier, Sir Austen Henry Layard had excavated in the ruins of Nineveh and published his two widely circulated and influential volumes, *Nineveh and its Remains* and *Discoveries in the Ruins of Nineveh and Babylon*.[4] European explorers, archaeologists, and adventurers were beginning systematically to collect Mesopotamian antiquities for museums in Europe, at the same time as American missionaries were actively seeking Assyrian reliefs and tablets to distribute to American university collections, museums, and learned societies.[5]

Salisbury's major source for his iconographic analysis was the work of the French diplomat and Orientalist Félix Lajard, whose publications were less sensational than Layard's and are today mostly forgotten. Salisbury, however, had in his personal library Lajard's work on Persian and Roman Mithraism, as well as his extensive study of the "pyramidal cypress" motif,[6] which Salisbury recognized on one of the Assyrian seals. Otherwise, Salisbury had few studies to inform him, and he was forced to rely mainly on formal resemblance.

Salisbury proposed that the theme of both cylinder seals was the "union of the male and female principles in the supreme divinity of the Assyrians."[7] Although he discreetly avoided any explicit terminology, his interpretation built upon the phallic appearance of the incense burner in seal no. 2, and the yonic appearance of a rhombic symbol present in both seals. Thus, he writes of seal no. 2: "*That the sacred fire and the moon, together, here symbolize the male and female principles, is partly indicated by the symbol* [the yonic rhomb] *beneath the moon, while the shape of the altar itself completes the expression of the idea.*"[8]

The seals have received scant scholarly attention in the 160 years since Salisbury's publication, beyond being included in the catalogues of Digard and Watanabe.[9] It is unclear when the seals made their way from the American Oriental Society to the Yale Babylonian Collection, but it is likely that they were transferred by Ferris J. Stephens in the 1940s or 1950s, during his tenure as both Curator of the Yale Babylonian Collection and Secretary-Treasurer of the American Oriental Society. The seals were photographed and catalogued on file cards for the Babylonian Collection by seal expert Briggs Buchanan in the 1960s.

They appear in the present volume for the first time with full descriptions and images.

SEAL 1: Red-brown limestone, 30×13mm, Neo-Assyrian, linear style. Probably ninth or early eighth century BCE.

(Photography by Carl Kaufman)

The seal shows an antithetical scene of a winged disc above a stylized tree, flanked by two nearly identical human worshippers. They are dressed in short-sleeved tunics, decorated by a fringe above the ankles. Over the tunic is draped a fringed shawl. They both wear a cap and have long beards and shoulder-length hair.

The winged disc has feathers flaring from a circle around a central drill-hole. It is topped by a double-hooked arch, and streamers extend from below the wings. This type occurs often on Assyrian linear style seals of soft stone and suggests a ninth- or early eighth-century dating.[10] The tree consists of a central tripartite trunk, with triangular branches all the way around. Nabu's wedge/stylus is placed to the right of the tree, and the enigmatic rhomb motif appears to the left.

The tree and winged disc are the focus of worship for the two humans, whose right hands reach toward the streamers extending from the winged disc, and whose left hands are raised in worship.

The scene is bordered top and bottom by a single line.

SEAL 2: Chalcedony, 32×11mm, Neo-Assyrian, drilled style.
Probably late eighth century BCE.

(Photography by Carl Kaufman)

A seated goddess, Ishtar or Gula, wearing a tall globe-topped(?) headdress (partly obscured by a chip) and a fringed robe, holds a ringlet in her left hand and extends her right hand. She sits on a chair whose high back is ornamented by three drill-holes. She faces a bearded, human worshipper approaching from the left. He wears a long robe with a fringe above his ankles and a rounded cap and extends both his hands in a gesture mirroring that of the goddess.

A rhomb is placed between him and an incense burner, with rising smoke indicated by two diverging sets of parallel lines. Above the incense burner to the left is a crescent and to the right the seven-star motif, *sebittu*.

In the terminus is a simple winged disc, with wings and tail consisting of parallel, horizontal lines. Below it are Nabu's wedge/stylus and Marduk's spade.

The scene and style find parallels among Assyrian hard-stone banquet seals dating to the late eighth century.[11]

The scene is bordered top and bottom by a single line.

NOTES

1. Edward E. Salisbury, "Remarks on Two Assyrian Cylinders Received from Mosûl," *Journal of the American Oriental Society* 5 (1856).

2. *Journal of the American Oriental Society* 5 (1856): xxxv–xxxvi.

3. Cf. the letter from Rev. William F. Williams, quoted by Sam Harrelson, *"Asia Has Claims Upon New England": Assyrian Reliefs at Yale* (New Haven: Yale University Art Gallery, 2006), 21.

4. Austen Henry Layard, *Nineveh and Its Remains* (New York: George P. Putnam, 1849); *Discoveries in the Ruins of Nineveh and Babylon* (London: John Murray, 1853).

5. Harrelson, *"Asia Has Claims Upon New England": Assyrian Reliefs at Yale*.

6. M. Félix Lajard, *Introduction á l'étude de culte public et des mystères de Mithra en Orient et en Occident* (Paris: Imprimerie royale, 1847); *Recherches sur le culte du cyprès pyramidal chez les peuples civilisés de l'antiquité* (Paris: Imprimerie royale, 1854).

7. Salisbury, "Remarks on Two Assyrian Cylinders Received from Mosûl," 192.

8. Ibid., 193.

9. Françoise Digard, *Répertoire analytique des cylindres Orientaux*, 3 vols. (Paris: Éditions du Centre national de la recherche scientifique, 1975), nos. 4716 and 4717; Kazuko Watanabe, "Seals of Neo-Assyrian Officials," in *Priest and Officials in the Ancient Near East*, ed. Watanabe (Heidelberg: Universitätsverlag C. Winter, 1999), no. 2.1.10.

10. Dominique Collon, *Cylinder Seals V: Neo-Assyrian and Neo-Babylonian Periods*, Catalogue of the Western Asiatic Seals in the British Museum (London: British Museum Press, 2001), 81.

11. Ibid., 65–67.

CONTRIBUTORS

Gojko Barjamovic
Department of Near Eastern Languages and Civilizations
Harvard University
Cambridge, MA 02138
barjamovic@fas.harvard.edu

Benjamin R. Foster
Department of Near Eastern Languages and Civilizations
Yale University
New Haven, CT 06520
benjamin.foster@yale.edu

Karen Polinger Foster
Departments of Near Eastern Languages and Civilizations and History of Art
Yale University
New Haven, CT 06520
karen.foster@yale.edu

Eckart Frahm
Department of Near Eastern Languages and Civilizations
Yale University
New Haven, CT 06520
eckart.frahm@yale.edu

Agnete Wisti Lassen
Yale Babylonian Collection
Yale University
New Haven, CT 06520
agnete.lassen@yale.edu

Suzanne L. Marchand
Department of History
Louisiana State University
Baton Rouge, LA 70803
smarch1@lsu.edu